Memories of Kreisau and the German Resistance

Memories of Kreisau and the German Resistance

(*Erinnerungen an Kreisau*)

Freya von Moltke

Translated and with an
introduction by Julie M. Winter

University of Nebraska Press
Lincoln and London

Originally published as *Erinnerungen an Kreisau, 1930–1945,*
© 1997 by C. H. Beck'sche Verlagsbuchhandlung, München
Translation, introduction, and glossary © 2003 by the University of Nebraska Press
Manufactured in the United States of America

Library of Congress Cataloging-in-Publication Data
Moltke, Freya von. [Erinnerungen an Kreisau, 1930–1945. English]
Memories of Kreisau and the German resistance
(Erinnerungen an Kreisau) / Freya von Moltke ;
translated by Julie M. Winter.
p. cm.
Includes bibliographical references.
ISBN 0-8032-4669-2 (cloth : alk. paper)
1. Moltke, Freya von.
2. Moltke, Helmuth James, Graf von, 1907–1945.
3. Kreisauer Kreis.   I. Title.
DD247.M595 A313 2003
943.086'092–dc21
2002013306

ISBN 0-8032-9625-8 (pbk. : alk. pa.)

Contents

Illustrations

Introduction

The fact that there was a significant German resistance to Hitler's regime has only recently gained wider notice in the English-speaking world. In addition to the comprehensive works published in English about the subject by Ger van Roon, Peter Hoffmann, and others, we are fortunate to have the personal memoirs, translated into English, of some of the resisters.[1] In the following memoir Freya von Moltke writes about her life in the resistance with her husband, Helmuth James von Moltke, a cofounder of the Kreisau Circle.

Freya von Moltke was born in 1911 in Cologne, Germany, to Ada and Carl Theodor Deichmann. In 1930 she began to study law in Bonn and in 1935 received her doctorate of law. In 1931 she married Helmuth James Count von Moltke and settled with him on his Silesian estate, Kreisau, located in present-day Poland. They had two sons, born in 1937 and 1941.[2] Freya helped run the von Moltke farm and grew to love her husband's Silesian homeland, family, and friends.

Helmuth James Count von Moltke, the great-great nephew of the famous German field marshal Helmuth von Moltke, was born in 1907 in Kreisau and grew up there with his four siblings. His mother, Dorothy Rose-Innes, was the daughter of the South African supreme court chief justice Sir James Rose-Innes. Helmuth James studied law from 1927 to 1929 and took over the management of the family farm in 1929. He was able to save it from financial ruin. In 1932 he and Freya moved to Berlin, where he opened his own practice specializing in international law. At this time he also underwent training to become a barrister in

England. After the birth of their children, Freya spent most of her time at Kreisau. Helmuth James was there as much as possible. Helmuth James was drafted into the German army in 1939; he served at the High Command of the Armed Forces as a specialist in martial law and international law. Beginning early in his law practice he helped Jews escape from Germany, and during his military service he worked for the humane treatment of prisoners of war by Germany. He also attempted to make the activities of the German resistance known abroad.

Vehemently opposed to the Nazi regime since its inception, Helmuth James sought like-minded people and by 1940 had begun to have regular discussions with them. He and Peter Yorck, an attorney and civil servant, are considered the cofounders and leaders of the Kreisau Circle. The inner circle of the resistance group consisted of about twenty members and included clergy, socialists, economic experts, and diplomats. In their numerous discussions, several taking place at the Moltke family estate in Kreisau, they planned for the reconstruction and governance of Germany after the collapse of the Third Reich.

Although Helmuth James and Peter Yorck did not originally believe in taking direct action against Hitler, by 1943 they realized that he had to be killed. The prime motivation for this change of position was their realization that the Nazi regime was systematically murdering Jews. In the fall of 1943 Col. Claus Stauffenberg, a cousin of Peter Yorck and the leader of the military resistance, joined the Kreisau group. A plan evolved in which Stauffenberg would assassinate Hitler by planting explosives near him. Both Yorck and Helmuth James thought that Stauffenberg had a good chance of succeeding. Helmuth James was arrested, however, on 19 January 1944, for warning a friend that he was about to be arrested, a matter completely unrelated to the conspiracy.[3]

On 20 July 1944 Col. Stauffenberg carried out the assassination attempt.[4] As a member of the General Staff, Stauffenberg was frequently in close proximity to Hitler. Early on the morning of 20 July Stauffenberg flew from Berlin to Hitler's headquarters in Wolfschanze. He brought along two sets of explosives with delay fuses. He and his aide were interrupted when trying to set the fuses and managed to set only one of them. Stauffenberg left the explosives in his briefcase under the table in the room where Hitler met with his staff, and was able to leave the compound with his aide. When he heard the huge explosion from the briefing hut a few minutes later, he assumed Hitler was dead. Had Stauffenberg been able to set both fuses, there is no doubt that everyone in the room would have been killed; however, Hitler survived with only minor injuries. Stauffenberg returned to Berlin intent on carrying out the coup. There, at army headquarters, Yorck was waiting for him as planned. The confusion that arose when it became clear that Hitler was not dead undermined the efforts of the conspirators. By midnight the revolt had collapsed, and Stauffenberg and three other members of the military resistance were accused of high treason, arrested, and immediately executed.

Shortly thereafter Yorck and other members of the inner circle of the Kreisau Circle were arrested, tried, and executed as well. Helmuth James was executed on 23 January 1945. In all, almost two hundred resisters were executed in connection with the 20 July 1944 coup attempt.[5]

Many of the Kreisau wives, among them Freya von Moltke, knew what their husbands were planning and supported them fully. Freya asserts in an interview: "I carried Helmuth's commitment with him from the beginning, and therefore, I wanted him to continue. . . . I never advised him to stop, but rather encouraged him, because I was convinced that that was the right way for him to fulfill his life."[6] In addition to her unwavering support, she helped with the meetings at Kreisau by providing food and hospitality. She was able to hide many of Helmuth James's letters, as well as documents pertaining to the work of the Kreisau Circle; she later smuggled them out of Silesia. She has published much of this material, and it is a valuable source of our knowledge of the activities of the Circle.

In her memoir, which is rich in detail, Freya gives an account of day-to-day life at the family estate before, during, and after the Nazi dictatorship. She writes about the von Moltke family, the Kreisau villagers, and the workers who helped run the farm, and she describes the beautiful Silesian countryside in a way that reveals that it had become a part of her. Furthermore, she outlines in detail the three meetings of the Kreisau Circle which took place at the estate and describes the participants and the work accomplished in the meetings. In the final chapter she writes about her life with the children after her husband was executed and how she attempted to hold onto the family estate.

Her memoir provides a very personal insight into the struggle against a totalitarian dictatorship under the ever-present threat of being charged with treason. Freya von Moltke now lives in Vermont and continues her efforts to foster a greater awareness of the work, the ideas, and the sacrifice of the members of the Kreisau Circle.

NOTES

1. Some excellent sources in English on the German resistance are Ger van Roon, *German Resistance to Hitler: Count von Moltke and the Kreisau Circle*, trans. Peter Ludlow (London: Van Nostrand Reinhold, 1971); Peter Hoffmann, *The History of the German Resistance: 1933–1945*, 3d ed., trans. Richard Barry (Montreal: McGill-Queen's University Press, 1996); David Clay Large, ed., *Contending with Hitler: Varieties of German Resistance in the Third Reich* (Washington DC: German Historical Institute and Cambridge University Press, 1991).

For a first-person account of the resistance, see Marion Yorck von Wartenburg, *The Power of Solitude: My Life in the German Resistance*, trans. Julie M. Winter (Lincoln: University of Nebraska Press, 2000).

2. For biographical information on Freya von Moltke and Helmuth James von Moltke, see Dorothee von Meding, *Mit dem Mut des Herzens: Die Frauen des 20. Juli* (Goldmann, 1997), 127–30.

3. Peter Hoffmann, "The Development of the German Resistance to Hitler," introduction to *Power of Solitude,* by Yorck von Wartenburg.

4. The following account is based on Peter Hoffmann, *Stauffenberg: A Family History, 1905–1944* (Cambridge: Cambridge University Press, 1995), 265–77.

5. Hoffmann, "Development of the German Resistance," xxvi.

6. von Meding, *Mit dem Mut des Herzens*, 134–35.

Wilhelm Viggo von Moltke, Helmuth James von Moltke, Asta von Moltke, and Freya von Moltke sit with the American journalist Edgar Mowrer and his daughter on the steps of the Berghaus.

Central Germany and Eastern Europe in 1930

Memories of Kreisau and the German Resistance

The Kreisau Circle

Ernst von Borsig
Alfred Delp (executed 1945)
Horst von Einsiedel
Otto Heinrich von der Gablentz
Eugen Gerstenmaier
Hans Bernd von Haeften (executed 1944)
Theo Haubach (executed 1945)
Paulus van Husen
Lothar Koenig
Julius Leber (executed 1945)
Hans Lukaschek
Carlo Mierendorff
Freya von Moltke
Helmuth James von Moltke (executed 1945)
Hans Carl Maria Alfons Peters
Harald Poelchau
Adolf Reichwein (executed 1944)
Eduard Waetjen
Irene Yorck von Wartenburg
Marion Yorck von Wartenburg
Peter Yorck von Wartenburg (executed 1944)

Life in Kreisau

In the spring of 1930, when I was just nineteen years old, I went with my brother Hans Deichmann to Kreisau for the first time. It was 911 kilometers by train from Cologne to Kreisau. That's what it said on my ticket. We were picked up at the Kreisau train station by Helmuth in a small green car, a so-called Opelfrosch, even though it was only a ten-minute walk to the *Berghaus* [mountain house], the comfortable family residence where the Moltke family was now living. There wasn't really a mountain—the house was situated somewhat elevated off to one side; a five-minute walk across meadows and farm fields and the small river Peile separated it from the farmyard, which lay in the middle of the village. I had never seen anything like it in the western part of Germany: an enormous, rectangular farmyard, framed by spacious, beautiful buildings, stables and barns with red-tiled roofs. The manor house, called the *Schloss* [palace], was also situated on the farmyard. At one time—as one can see in old pictures—it had the proportions of a beautiful, large eighteenth-century country house. And that's what it was still like when the old field marshal Helmuth von Moltke lived there. In 1867 Moltke, while serving as chief of the Prussian General Staff, had acquired the former estate Kreisau with its outlying farms in Nieder Gräditz and Wierischau from a family by the name of von Dresky, using a cash endowment granted to him by the Prussian king.

The endowment represented Prussia's gratitude for the battle Moltke won against the Austrians near Königgrätz in Bohemia. Through renovations, additions, and reconstruction, the next generation modernized and enlarged the manor, until it became an enormous, imposing box. However, the field marshal's room was preserved. In fact, it became a place of pilgrimage for many Germans, dutifully shown over and over again by members of the Moltke family. The memory of the field marshal was a matter of respect in the family but nothing more than that.

Later during financially difficult times, it became prohibitive to heat the big house in the winter, and so in 1928 the family moved to the Berghaus. The field marshal had previously settled his widowed sister-in-law there, and this house had always been a part of Moltke family life. Now it was brought to life again and, rightly so, loved again. The manor, however, did not remain completely uninhabited. Sections of it, which could be heated with stoves, were rented and lived in, at least in the summers, by widowed aunts. Now the situation was reversed: widowed aunts lived in the manor, the Moltkes in the Berghaus.

The Opelfrosch, which, by the way, I never saw again after our first visit, took us there. We never again owned a car in Kreisau.

At this point Dorothy von Moltke was living in the Berghaus with her five children, including, since the end of 1929, the son she admired, Helmuth James. When difficult times progressed into an acute catastrophe for the farm, the father Helmuth called for help from his twenty-two-year-old eldest son, who, after having passed his first-stage law examinations, was working in a bank in Berlin. Father Helmuth made Helmuth James his general representative and completely withdrew from the Kreisau business. At that time Father Helmuth was already living mainly in Berlin. In his youth he had been healed of a serious ailment through Christian Science, the teachings of an American Christian denomination. Not only did he remain a follower of this group his whole life, but he also became very active in it by performing and teaching healings. His work for Christian Science developed more and more into a professional activity, and Christian Science, which understands healing as a spiritual responsibility, played a major role in Helmuth James's parents' generation. However, the next generation did not adopt this religion. The younger Helmuth had himself confirmed by the old pastor in the large neighboring village of Gräditz.

The Kreisau Moltkes had closer ties to Berlin, even though it was 250 kilometers away, than to Breslau, only 50 kilometers away. Again and again they had taken up residence in Berlin, and so it remained. This had developed quite naturally, for as legal successors to the field marshal, who had no children himself, the following two generations of Kreisau Moltkes were members of the Prussian Upper Chamber until it was dissolved in 1918.

The elder Helmuth had employed an agronomist to administer the farm. This man died suddenly at the end of September 1929, and it became evident that he must have been sick for a while, or at least not up to the job. Without the knowledge of the owner, he had run up considerable new debts on the farm, which was already deep in debt; he had entered into unrealizable contracts; the whole business was in a financial shambles. Bankruptcy proceedings and a judgment in favor of the creditors, which would mean the loss of the farm, were imminent. Through laborious effort Helmuth James set about to make order out of the chaos and to set up a plan for the creditors, mainly banks, making it appear more attractive for them to continue to manage the farm, rather than forcing it to be sold at an auction. At the time of the economic crisis, 1930–31, it probably would have been impossible to get a fair price for the property anyway. Helmuth James—the lawyer—transformed the farm into a Kreisau corporation run for the benefit of the creditors. He acquired a new man, Adolf Zeumer, to administer the farm. Zeumer and Helmuth James became employees of the company. The owner and the rest of his family no longer had any claims to the income. They received only "payment in kind": milk, butter, flour, potatoes, and whatever else the farm produced. In order to help out with cash income, Dorothy von Moltke took in people from England who wanted to learn German and who stayed for many months.

Sixty years earlier the field marshal had wanted his family to resettle to a life on the land. His father had lost land several times. He himself had grown up in very dire conditions. He looked around in Silesia and liked Kreisau. No wonder. It lies nestled in a valley in the beautiful undulating farmland of central Silesia between the Eule Mountains and the Zobten—the mountains on the horizon. On the upper edge of the valley runs one of the old roads, which earlier connected the east to the west. Large farms alternate with narrow cultivated strips of land, and among them are meadows and shrub forests. The land has a magnificent expanse, and above it is a big bright sky. The Eule Mountains, one thousand meters high and belonging to the Sudetenland, dominate the landscape with their gentle lines in the distance. Kreisau has a continental climate, that is, long, cold winters. There is not always snow, but I do remember beautiful excursions in the horse-drawn sled. Dry, warm summers followed.

When we arrived at Kreisau in the spring of 1930, the mood in the Berghaus was quite relaxed, in spite of the difficult situation. Of course we went to visit Helmuth, to get to know his family, and to see his homeland. I had met Helmuth and his brother Joachim Wolfgang for the first time the previous summer, during a unique vacation with Dr. Eugenie Schwarzwald, the famous Vienna pedagogue and philanthropist who used to rent an empty hotel for her many friends at Grundlsee in the Salzkammergut in Austria. Now my brother and I immediately, and gladly, fell under the spell of Helmuth's mother, Dorothy von Moltke, née Rose Innes. She was the only child of the first "präsidierenden Richters" (chief justice) of the Supreme Court of the South African Union, Sir James Rose Innes, and his energetic, intelligent wife Jessie, née Pringle. Both parents came from Scottish families who had emigrated to South Africa in the 1820s. South Africa had become part of the British Commonwealth. Dorothy's parents felt themselves to be members of this large union, but above all, they were South Africans. Mother and daughter Rose Innes, during an educational tour for the young daughter in Europe, had departed from Dresden for a summer break in the country at Kreisau. They were enticed by an advertisement of the enterprising mistress of Kreisau at the time, Ella, née Countess Bethusy Huc. She was the wife of Wilhelm von Moltke, who had inherited Kreisau from the childless field marshal in 1891. "Mother Ella," whom I unfortunately never met, was enterprising in a number of ways—in Kreisau it supposedly even came to table moving and spiritual séances. Legend had it that during a séance she learned that happiness would come to Kreisau in the form of a young woman. She would make her first appearance wearing a white dress and a blue necklace. In any case, it is said that on the first evening of her visit

Dorothy was wearing a white dress and a string of blue beads around her neck. And so it was that the parents of Helmuth James met. I wonder if Father Helmuth sang himself into Dorothy's heart, for his singing was so captivatingly beautiful, and he could have become a great singer. Unfortunately, I heard him sing on only one occasion.

After Dorothy's first visit things still took a while. There was some ambivalence. The South African parents did not gladly see their daughter disappear into eastern Germany. At that time it meant being separated from her by a three-week ship voyage; there were not yet any airplanes or telephones that could function across such distances. But in 1905, soon after the sudden death of Wilhelm von Moltke, Dorothy became the next mistress of Kreisau. Indeed she brought a lot of joy to the family in Kreisau, for with her sincere warmth, her candor, and her readiness to devote herself to others, she became the focal point of this large family and of the hospitable household through which so many guests passed. She was greatly loved. Into this world, which was completely new to her, she brought along her own opinions about people and things and a very lively interest in public affairs.

We could feel that immediately. In spite of the straitened circumstances, Dorothy lived very happily in the Berghaus, enjoying her five growing children. Her husband came for visits. She was free of the big household in the manor, and a happy, cosmopolitan atmosphere prevailed. The connection with South Africa was never broken. Letters went back and forth each week. Parents and daughter saw each other at least every two years. There was an especially close relationship between father and daughter. Dorothy's father had been a lawyer at first, then a liberal politician and a minister of justice before being appointed a judge. Both directly and indirectly through his daughter he had a great influence on his grandson Helmuth James and his concept of justice.

In any case, we ate South African biltong—dried, grated antelope meat—on our bread at breakfast, which of course we Rhinelanders found fascinating; and we were happy to sit at the big round table in the dining room of the Berghaus with the family. Joachim Wolfgang, next eldest after Helmuth James, was studying art history. Willo had just completed his high school examinations; he wanted to become an architect and was doing a practical-training year as a bricklayer in

Schweidnitz, the nearby district town. The two youngest, Carl Bernd and Asta, were still in school.

Because my heart was full of Helmuth, all of Kreisau also seemed irresistible to me. Everything was new for me. But at that time I was completely happy with anything that was part of Helmuth's world. After our visit we started writing letters to each other again.[1] Whoever wants to become acquainted with Helmuth, must read his letters. He is not easy to describe, especially not for me.

He described himself as a complicated person. He had a tall, slender figure—he was well over six feet tall and for that reason striking—and was dark-haired like his mother. He was considered reserved and as a person who kept his distance. But whoever could pick up the expression in his lively brown eyes would immediately sense his warmth. Perhaps only those closest to him could see this, as well as his cheerfulness. He liked to make fun of people closest to him but never in a hurtful way. And it was fun for him to shock people who were not so close to him. There was a photograph of him where he had posed with a hammer and sickle in his hands, although he never was a Communist. His conservative Pomeranian relatives thought that he was not worthy of being the heir of Kreisau. Along with his friends and family I believed in his great talents. In every task of life it was easy for him to make decisions. He understood how to give people direction, and he was trusted greatly. Although he himself was reserved, he was very open to the worries of his fellow human beings. His siblings were not the only ones who looked up to him.

I had begun to study law at the universities in Cologne and Bonn. We visited each other in western Germany, eastern Germany, and in Austria. It was a stressful and demanding year for Helmuth. The condition of the farm had been extremely muddled. It still required long, complicated negotiations, restructuring of the debt, and the making of new plans,

---

[1] Freya von Moltke, Michael Balfour, Julian Frisby, *Helmuth James Graf Moltke 1907–1945*. Berlin, 1984 (now Zurich, Diogenes Verlag). Helmuth James von Moltke, *Briefe an Freya 1939–1945*. Munich: C.H. Beck, 2nd edition, 1991. *Helmuth James Graf von Moltke, Letzte Briefe*. Zurich: Diogenes Verlag, 1997.

until the situation was more or less secure again; and it was several more years before the farm recovered completely. Hindenburg's "Eastern Relief" for the reconstruction of eastern German agriculture, which in general was in deep debt due to the great economic crisis, ultimately benefited Kreisau as well.

One day in Cologne in the summer of 1931, I received a letter from Helmuth. Since his mother wanted to go to South Africa for six months in the fall, and a replacement for her was needed in the house for the younger siblings, it would be best if we were to marry and I was to come to the Berghaus. And so it happened.

I was not at all a good catch, for quite shortly before our wedding my father's bank had "stopped payments." But Helmuth said we could live like two students—better together than alone. What I did bring along, however, was a Rhenish left-bank habit of independence, which I owed most of all to my upbringing by my two older brothers Carl and Hans and also to my mother. I also have the good fortune to come from a long line of women who moved about freely in life. I took this freedom as a given for myself, and I have never been disappointed in it. I was very warmly received in Kreisau.

I had few household duties, as those were in the hands of "Mamsell," Mrs. Ida Märkert. She was a widowed, childless farmer's wife, who had lost her farm, house, and money during the inflation, and therefore, though already advanced in years, worked as a cook at the Moltkes'. She had moved with them to the Berghaus, and there she once again had something like a farmhouse to care for. She looked after everything, in the house and the garden; young girls from the village helped. In Mamsell I got to know my first true Silesian woman. In Silesia I met other people of her kind, people who had great inner self-reliance and independence, unerring in their judgment. In spite of her dependent position now, she didn't lose her inner freedom to give her all with joy, and that she did. Mamsell was friends with all of us, but most of all with Helmuth James, and least of all with the father Helmuth, who thought she didn't cook well enough. I can still hear Helmuth James, as he came in from the farm, greeting Mamsell at the kitchen window with "Hail, Märkert," to which she accordingly replied, "Hail, Moltke."

Here I must also mention the parish sister and the soul of the village, Sister Ida Hübner, a deaconess from Frankenstein in Silesia. A kindergarten had been established by the field marshal for the children of working mothers in Kreisau; it was called the *Spielschule*. Many Kreisauers had passed through the school of wise Sister Ida. In addition she took care of the health of the village and also that of the Moltkes, who did not believe in doctors but rather in Sister Ida.

I had already studied law for a few semesters in Bonn, and now I was participating in some seminars in Breslau. Helmuth also employed me right away. During the first winter I worked out endless statistics for him about the unemployed in the Waldenburg coal-mining area. The miserable conditions under which the miners in Waldenburg were still forced to live had bothered Helmuth for years. Again and again he tried to get the word out about the inhumane conditions. He even brought famous American journalists, who were his friends, to Waldenburg so that they could write about it.

The farm was once again running in an orderly manner under Adolf Zeumer's strict and efficient supervision. He was generally respected. From early till late he went with his horse and a light two-wheeled cart—called a "spider"—to the various work sections, over fields and meadows, from one end of the farm to the other. It was said that whenever something went wrong anywhere, Herr Zeumer immediately appeared with his horse on the horizon, as if summoned. He was also an independent man and not easy going. He had previously run his wife's farm, but the operation of a larger agricultural business, indeed the task of rebuilding the Moltkes' run-down farm business, had probably also appealed to him. He and Helmuth James worked together very well until [Helmuth's death in] 1945.

The soil in Kreisau is only of average quality and is very uneven. There are the sandy terminal moraines of the Eule Mountains—only oats and rye grow there. The more demanding agricultural crops—wheat, barley, sugar beets, and potatoes—thrive in Kreisau's richer soil. Twelve hundred acres were "under the plow," and in addition there were four hundred acres of paddocks—that is, meadows and woods. Under the impressive arches of the large barn were about sixty cows, and there were also young cattle. The milk was taken daily in a horse-pulled cart to the dairy in Schweidnitz. Approximately one hundred pigs were fattened, and their piglets were raised also in Kreisau. During the war we acquired a large herd of sheep, two hundred ewes. When I came to Kreisau, all the work in the field was still carried out with teams of horses. Gradually we were able to buy machines that were more modern. With careful tending the farm was able to properly nourish the animals and the people who lived and worked there. Up to sixty people worked on the farm in the high season, including the women, whose help in caring for the beets and the harvest was also important. Helmuth firmly controlled economic and financial matters, but as soon as possible he began to remove himself from an active position of control and continued the rest of his law training at the courts in Reichenbach and Schweidnitz.

I recall that during this first winter I had to learn to play bridge, for that was a very popular game in the family entertainment of the Moltke house. With Carl Bernd and Asta in the house there were four of us, as the game requires. It is an interesting game, and they all, even the young people, played it splendidly. I had to learn it and at first played badly and didn't like to lose, but all of it contributed to those idyllic winter evenings.

In the fall of 1932 we took an apartment in Berlin. It was tiny and was in an old building on Bendler—now Stauffenberg Strasse, right next to Tiergarten Park. For me it was simply magnificent to finally be able to live alone with Helmuth. The German training of a lawyer included six months of legal work at a law office and six months of legal work at a higher regional court. Helmuth wanted to do both in Berlin. He first worked in the law office of Koch-Weser and Carlebach, then at the Superior Court of Justice, the Berlin higher regional court. Nevertheless, Kreisau remained the ever-present, constant background in our life, always a place of yearning for all absent members of the family. Even while living in Berlin, we spent a lot of time in Kreisau. Helmuth continued to look after the farm and went to Silesia at least once a month.

We were in Berlin on 30 January 1933, the day on which Hindenburg named Hitler chancellor of the Reich. The former Landrat of Waldenburg, Dr. Ohle, a Social Democrat with whom Helmuth had worked during his efforts to relieve the suffering of the miners, was at our house for lunch. It was his opinion that one must allow the Nazis to come into power, so that they, like other governments at that time, would deteriorate and would then be replaced. Helmuth contradicted him despairingly and passionately—it was the beginning of a catastrophe of the worst kind. In the family we always discussed the political situation with emotion and anxiety. This was already true during the chaotic times, resembling civil war, that had preceded the Hitler government.

There was no trace left of the military tradition in the family. The Kreisauers—even Helmuth's father—felt themselves to be democrats and had a positive opinion of the Weimar Republic. They voted for the center parties. Helmuth, with his socialistic tendencies, was by far the most radical one. He regretted the weaknesses of the Reichstag and regarded Chancellor Brüning's policy of governing without the parliament, and with emergency decrees in accord with the emergency paragraphs of the Weimar constitution, as extremely dangerous to the survival of democracy. He had no doubts about Hitler's plans. He—but not I—had read and taken seriously Hitler's book, *Mein Kampf*. During the so-called National Socialist Gleichschaltung that enveloped Germany, Mamsell in Kreisau was asked to join the Nazi Women's Organization—actually a relatively harmless organization in comparison to others—and she refused, giving the reason "Herr von Moltke says Hitler means war."

In Kreisau Mamsell could get away with saying that. And we could also get away with a lot. Kreisau was a small village with only about four hundred inhabitants. Besides our farm, there were several other small farms; some members of these farms also worked in the district town Schweidnitz because they did not earn enough by farming. The Moltke family was respected. They never behaved in a "grand" way. I, at least, never experienced such a thing. They had a simple and modest lifestyle. It was known that they had not been doing well financially in the years before the Nazi period, and it probably was also known that Helmuth James, in his work of rebuilding, was able to fully take into account the claims of some farmers who had suffered losses because of our farm. There was something like a symbiosis in Kreisau. In any case, in the village there was astonishment rather than hostility toward the obvious fact that the Moltkes were not ready to allow themselves to be seized by National Socialism.

It became important for us that Herr Zeumer immediately and enthusiastically joined the Nazi Party, became head of the department, and thus controlled the police force in the village. He was a powerful man in Kreisau. In the years when Germans denounced each other by the thousands—even within families—and in so doing often brought each other into life-threatening danger, Herr Zeumer's loyalty protected us. Zeumer and Helmuth spoke again and again with each other about Nazi Germany. When Hindenburg ran for the office of Reich president for the second time, Helmuth considered him too old and the people around him too dangerous. Since no one else of importance was running, as a protest Helmuth decided—and I along with him— to vote for Thälmann, the Communist candidate, who did not have the slightest chance of being elected. So Zeumer asked Helmuth to vote in Berlin, not in Kreisau, for it would come out immediately that we were the ones who had voted for Thälmann. We followed his advice. Zeumer was always full of optimism that the Führer would take care of everything; he was never ready to see that Hitler wanted war and was preparing for it. Helmuth never concealed his fundamental opinions and his deep pessimism from Zeumer. Helmuth's pessimism simply never affected Zeumer. He had his hands full of things to do. He had important work—he didn't look right or left and simply trusted everything to the Führer. But Zeumer also didn't let anything happen to Helmuth. His respect for the Führer was balanced by his respect for Helmuth, although it was respect of a completely different kind. Helmuth, for his part, greatly esteemed Zeumer. He knew that he could depend on him.

Herr Zeumer's conduct was of great practical consequence to us. In small and large matters he stood between us and the Nazi Party. As an example, there was the matter of flying the flag. The flag had to be flown on all possible occasions. The Berghaus was situated out of the way. We did not live in the manor. The flag was only flown on the farm at Herr Zeumer's house, but that was enough. Of course there was also no "Heil Hitler" between him and us. Generally I was always able to get around that by greeting people first, and only a few—the true National Socialists—replied to me with the Hitler greeting.

There were other reasons why our Kreisau life protected us from the National Socialists. This was very important to Helmuth, who from the beginning to the end lived in deeply principled and active opposition to the regime. Kreisau conferred on us the honor of being the legal successor to Field Marshal von Moltke, who was highly esteemed by the National Socialists. Kreisau produced food, which was always needed and was later of importance to the war. The farm was so far out of the way and so small that by the time news made its way there, it was in a milder form; in short, Kreisau made us more independent than were many others who opposed the Nazi regime, and Helmuth was always aware of this.

In the first months of 1934 Helmuth took the licensing exam in Berlin, which made him a fully trained lawyer. Right after that we accepted an invitation from Helmuth's grandparents to go to South Africa. We stayed there for six months, and it was during these months that we—especially I—really made these strong wise people a part of our lives. On the way back to Europe Helmuth went to England for the first time in his life.

We were in Capetown on 30 June 1934 when, during the so-called Röhm-Putsch, the dastardly and unscrupulous murderous activities of the National Socialists became apparent abroad. Our new South African friends advised us to stay in South Africa. But we wanted to return to Germany—Helmuth and I were in agreement. We were both tied much too strongly to Germany, not only because Helmuth was responsible for Kreisau and its future legacy, but because he was also the oldest of the younger generation of a close-knit family and was in many respects leading the way. We were not yet among the persecuted. Besides, at that time Helmuth had probably already decided to remain in Germany as an opponent of the National Socialists or at least to stay on and, if possible, become active as an opponent.

After we returned, Helmuth had to figure out what he could do as a lawyer. It was out of the question for him to set up a practice as a lawyer in Schweidnitz, the district town located six kilometers from Kreisau. His opposition to the Nazi regime would have become too obvious

there. He wanted to be in a position to assist victims of the regime.
So he set up his law practice in Berlin, where his activities were not so
noticeable, and entered into a partnership with the international law
specialist Karl von Lewinski, an older attorney. They had a nice office
at 64 Unter den Linden. In addition, Helmuth looked for a legal way to
periodically get out of Germany. He found it in England by beginning
further legal study, which eventually made him a barrister (1939), one
of the two types of British lawyers. Only a barrister can plead a case in
court. In addition to passing the appropriate exams, the education of
a barrister required participation in three evening meals per semester
in the halls of one of the legal guilds. Every barrister-to-be in England
had to belong to one of these guilds, a rule preserved from the Middle
Ages. Like his South African grandfather, Helmuth became a member
of the "Inner Temple" guild and had to go at least three times a year to
"dinners" in London.

But that's not all—during his numerous visits to England he also
made many new friends. That's how his friendship originated with the
former Commonwealth politician Lionel Curtis and his wife, as well
as his friendship with Michael Balfour and his wife Grizel, friendships
that for me have also lasted a lifetime. Julian Frisby also belonged to
this group. He was one of the young men who had learned German
with Dorothy Moltke. After his first stay he came as a guest to Kreisau
every summer up until the war. Julian was completely at home with us.
He was a wonderful gardener and contributed a lot to the improvement
of the Berghaus garden. He collected butterflies and, for this purpose,
brought along his butterfly net from England. The fact that he, eccentric
as he was, would sometimes even wear green suede shoes, made it
impossible for Asta—fifteen years old at the time—to be seen with
him in Schweidnitz. Only the English produce such fine and lovable
eccentrics! All of these friendships contributed to the loving respect that
always prevailed in Kreisau for the British Commonwealth, which of
course at that time still included South Africa.

Kreisau's farming remained in the competent hands of Herr Zeumer.
But we traveled regularly to Kreisau. The afternoon train from Berlin
to Silesia left at around 5 P.M. One had to change trains in Liegnitz.
Several slower trains then went daily from there, along the mountains, to

Upper Silesia. That was a much traveled branch line. Kreisau, which was located between Schweidnitz and Reichenbach, became a permanent train station after the death of the field marshal, when the emperor disembarked there for his burial. However, the afternoon train from Berlin connected in Liegnitz to an express train, which didn't stop in Kreisau. So one had to get a taxi in Schweidnitz to arrive at home around 10:30 P.M.

There were good and not so good harvests; there were estimates that could either be met or not be met. The farm continued to thrive; it could pay its interest and continue to pay off its debt. Finally the corporation for the creditors was dissolved again. The farm was completely free of debt, but that wasn't until about the end of the war. When Helmuth told me about this final success I said, "Now either the Russians or the Nazis will get it." Helmuth replied, "Better with no debts!"

In 1935, however, the Moltke family was dealt a hard blow: the death of Dorothy von Moltke, who had just returned from a trip to South Africa. She probably died from a growth in her brain, but this could not be established with certainty. Her death was completely unexpected; she was only fifty-one years old. The domination of Germany by the National Socialists had struck to the core of her being. She had not easily acquired her loyalty to Germany, but she stood the test in the First World War. Now she had lost the Germany that she was ready to trust, and she knew that her children were in danger. We buried her solemnly and very sadly on the chapel hill with the participation of the whole village, the surrounding area, and the entire family; the women of the village sang. Dorothy's mother was also there; she had come back to Germany with her daughter to go to a spa.

The chapel hill, a wooded hill near the village, got its name from a small, modest chapel-like building of red brick built in the Gründerzeit style. The field marshal had had it built for himself and his wife, whom he'd buried there in 1868. He did not follow her until 1891. Since then a whole line of Moltkes has been buried there. In 1941, in the middle of the Second World War, we celebrated the fiftieth anniversary of the field marshal's death in the presence of a delegation of high-ranking officers and the extended family. On this occasion the Nazi Party wanted to replace the simple chapel with a more magnificent mausoleum. Helmuth James successfully opposed it on the grounds that this would not be in keeping with the wishes and the lifestyle of the one being honored.

From what I've written so far it is probably clear that the Moltkes did not live year-round at Kreisau, even though they were profoundly and firmly rooted there. Dorothy too, after her children no longer went to school in Reichenbach or Schweidnitz, lived with her husband in Berlin in the winter. After her death, her responsibilities for Kreisau and for the family fell to me, but even I was not permanently in Kreisau until after the birth of our older son, Helmuth Caspar (November 1937). Up to then I spent the winters with Helmuth James in Berlin, the summers in Kreisau. Whenever Helmuth was absent from Kreisau, I maintained the connection between him and the farm, mainly with detailed daily letters. Through these Helmuth lived in very close contact with Kreisau and the farm until his death.

I usually spent one work shift a day on the farm. That meant that I was alternately from 6 A.M. to 9 A.M., or from 9 A.M. to noon, or in the afternoon, sitting high up on the spider with Herr Zeumer. Over hill and dale it went, and I marvel in retrospect that I only fell off once—strangely enough on my last trip, but I'll tell about that later. I did take over parts of Helmuth's managerial functions at Kreisau during the war. These concerned the management of the finances, the planning of the crops, as well as the routine tracking of the work processes and the yields. I never made independent decisions in farm matters. I did not have the training or the experience to do that.

Helmuth's law practice in Berlin started up slowly. Along with his law cases Helmuth also found the opportunity to advise and assist emigrating Jews. From the very beginning he urged Jewish people to leave Germany without reservation. Holland would not be far enough away. Close personal, dear, and well-loved friends of ours were also affected. For example, Helmuth gave advice to the family of my great law professor, Martin Wolff, and such activities often went on for years.

In view of the extent of the terrible crimes committed later by the National Socialists, but inevitably also in the name of and with the help of a so-called cultured nation, which considered itself to be humane and progressive, it often goes unnoticed that the persecution of Jews in Germany went through many stages. That happened not out of consideration for the Jews but rather out of consideration for what non-Jewish Germany and foreign countries would tolerate. In the first years of the Nazi regime no one could have imagined what it would come to. But there was a lot of depressing work. For Helmuth life in Berlin became more and more unbearable from year to year. It was an agonizing mixture of knowledge about what was going on and the direction in which it was developing—a knowledge, which he knew how to obtain and wanted to obtain—and the realization that he was relatively unable to do anything about it. After 1 December 1938, he was not allowed to officially represent Jews, so after that he did it illegally.

Helmuth's father died in 1939, and Helmuth inherited Kreisau. In the meantime, Nazi Germany had experienced a great upswing and enjoyed one foreign policy success after the other. There were new jobs, things were going better for many people, and Germany was becoming more powerful. Rearmament, the elimination of the Jews, the violent extermination of any opposition, the Gleichschaltung of the whole country—that was the stuff of the years before the war. The methods were brutal. Beginning in February and March 1933 there were no longer any legal rights; first the fundamental rights of the individual were revoked by emergency decree, and then the constitution was abolished by the Reichstag itself. Whatever served the Nazi regime was right. The terrible concentration camps were built originally for German opponents of National Socialism. Many were either murdered there without further ado or were condemned to death by means of so-called normal proceedings. However, the murdering on a grand scale did not begin until the war.

In the years before the war, we who were not yet being persecuted continued to live relatively unmolested. In spite of his law practice in Berlin and his studies in England, Helmuth was in Kreisau a lot—in the beautiful Kreisau that was being reconstructed. It made him happy to see the fertile farm prosper. We wandered time and again over the peaceful countryside, over the fields and meadows and through the bush, as the Silesians called the small wooded areas that lay between the fields. How wonderful, for example, was the scent of the freshly plowed soil and of the lilies of the valley in the woods! How wonderful to observe the growing, blooming, ripening! Year in, year out, walking alone with Helmuth for hours over the fields—those are my happiest memories of life in Kreisau.

Kreisau also made it possible for us to be hospitable. It was common that people—and not only our closer family members—came and went, staying for short or long periods with us. Even the village was used to that. We conducted a country household—in the Berghaus and also in the big house on the farm, the household of the aunts with their children and grandchildren. There was plenty of help. We had a good life in the comfortable Berghaus and on its large, covered veranda overlooking the garden, where we took our meals from breakfast to supper in summer. The garden, in which all of us worked, especially Helmuth, had, of course, a fruit and vegetable section, which provided for us. Then during the war we added bees. You could no longer buy honey, which Helmuth really liked. For that reason I learned, from two old Silesians, how to keep bees. One of the two sold me the hives with which I began. The old beekeepers had an easier time of it than I did, for they held pipes in the corners of their mouths and blew smoke on the bees to keep them away. In spite of that I never did take up their habit of pipe smoking. In these years Helmuth enjoyed more of what was going on in the beehives—which filled our letters—than the honey that they finally produced. Once I also sent to him in Berlin a dead queen bee. He had never seen one, and even I'd had a great deal of trouble trying to find and kill one in a wild swarm, which actually should not have been swarming at all. Without the queen such a swarm immediately returns to its home.

It is difficult to convey that this still peaceful life really took place against a background of latent danger. Whoever opposed the ruling dictatorship and expressed or showed it through his actions, had to count on at least a period of time in a concentration camp. Life-threatening danger was always present and fear contributed to keeping people under control. Why did we personally never live in a condition of fear? Probably because we so firmly believed in the necessity of what we undertook. Danger became a part of everyday life.

Life in the Berghaus remained peaceful for a long time, even though by the beginning of the war the type of visitors we had changed somewhat. But the extent of the comings and goings remained about the same. More people were coming to recuperate, to eat, and to get away from the bombs. Helmuth met the outbreak of the war in the Berghaus by taking care that no type of weapon was kept in the house. Weapons in the house during war could only cause their wrongful use. I never saw hunting rifles in the Berghaus anyway. The hunt had long since been leased to some doctors in the district town of Schweidnitz for financial reasons. When I found two old pistols, I threw them into the Peile River.

Our Work for the Future

War! That terrible war of enslavement and extermination, for which the Nazis had been preparing since the very first day. Always looming from 1938 on, by us always profoundly hated and feared, it was finally started by Nazi Germany's invasion of Poland. This could potentially be the beginning of the end of the National Socialist dictatorship in Europe. Helmuth had rarely doubted that. But what enormous sacrifices there would be in this war! In the end it turned out as Helmuth had expected. However, time and again it could have gone either way. "Even if Hitler conquers England," Helmuth asserted, "the English will not give in. The king and the government will go to Canada, and the United States will enter the war. In the end Germany will be defeated." And that was just the West! Then the East came into the picture. For the future of humanity on earth, one had to wish that the Germans would be defeated, if it were not possible to destroy from the inside a regime still approved of by a majority of Germans.

And then what? Thinking about this question and that there really would be an "afterward," however things should turn out, gave many people the courage to continue living at that time. Even before the war there were the beginnings of conversations about this topic in Helmuth's circle of friends. This was true for Eduard Waetjen, an attorney, Horst von Einsiedel, and Carl Dietrich von Trotha, Helmuth's cousin. Although Waetjen later left Germany, he participated in these conversations until 1943; after that he tried to help the Kreisauers from Switzerland. The other two, together with Trotha's splendid wife

Margrit, became highly active participants during the war years, even though they always remained in the background.

It wasn't until January 1940 that they began to systematically deal with this topic. That is when Peter Yorck and Helmuth met each other again after a long time and found themselves in agreement. They met in the inviting small row house of the Yorcks (50 Hortensienstrasse, Berlin-Lichterfelde), whose narrow, long garden ran up against the tracks of the city train. The first step—the search for people who were ready to participate in such a thing—received its real impetus with the German victory over France in the summer of 1940, at the pinnacle of German success in the war, rather than later when it was clear that Germany would lose the war. At that time it was truly an act of faith to occupy oneself with the time after the war and certainly also an act of self-preservation, the preservation of one's own integrity. It was probably at this point in time that Helmuth and I, between ourselves, explicitly decided to carry this commitment together.

At first this had nothing to do with Kreisau. Helmuth was drafted at the beginning of the Polish campaign by the High Command of the Armed Forces, Counter-Intelligence Service, Foreign Division, as an expert in martial law and international public law. He didn't come back to Kreisau for the first time until Christmas, and after that the visits were further and further apart. However, from time to time during the course of the war I was able to visit him for a weekend in Berlin. Helmuth's only sister, Asta, made that possible.

Asta, who had been working as an interior designer in Berlin, came back to Kreisau at the outbreak of the war to avoid the possibility of being drafted to do another kind of war work. She worked for a good while on the farm. Since many of our best workers became soldiers, she drove the tractor in Kreisau for a long time. This meant that she sat on her tractor and pulled the appropriate equipment over the land that was to be tilled; she plowed, she harrowed, she sowed—whatever was needed. During the war it became a burning question as to what manpower would be available for the farm. As early as the summer of 1940 Zeumer went to Poland—he spoke Polish—to recruit voluntary workers. After that several Polish families moved to Kreisau. Every year around Christmas they returned to Poland, and each time we worried about whether they would return in time for the spring tilling. In fact, they did return every year. All these families were still in Kreisau when Silesia became Polish, and we had to leave.

During the war a work camp was established in the large neighboring village of Grädirz. At first French prisoners of war were housed there. When our workload was heavy, some of these prisoners also worked for us. Later, Russian prisoners of war arrived; they seemed to be treated worse, and so we made soup for them at noon on the farm. The Russians did not stay long with us. Finally, there were also Jews in the work camp. They never worked for us, but for a while we saw them in Kreisau at the Peile River. This river sometimes caused great floods in the whole area, which was to be remedied by changing its course. The Jews wore the striped uniforms of concentration camp inmates and were watched by a Jew—he also wore concentration camp clothing. We did not yet know that they were doing work that would ultimately end with their deaths.

Asta's presence in Kreisau made it possible for me to occasionally go to Berlin, where I met, and grew to highly regard, most of the people who were ready to participate in the plans for the time after Nazism. Helmuth valued my opinion about people. After all, it was a question of trust in the first degree. One day he asked me whether Konrad Adenauer, whom I had gotten to know when he was mayor of Cologne through his friendly relationship with my mother, was suited to work with them in this group. My answer proves how young we were, for I said that he was already too old for that! I was truly surprised and impressed by the variety and quality of the men whom I met at that time—each one of them had special knowledge and experience to bring to the discussion. In this way I also met Berthold Stauffenberg, Claus Stauffenberg's older brother, an attorney specializing in international law. He was a quiet, reflective, serious, and ponderous sort of person and, in contrast to his younger brother, not at all soldierly. In Berlin he had similar war duties as Helmuth at the High Command of the Armed Forces. He did not take part in the work of the Kreisau Circle.

A close friendship developed between the Yorcks and us; it was an especially nice relationship, which was very precious to us over the years. When weighing the importance of the members within the Kreisau

Circle, Peter Yorck's role has always been underestimated. The reason for that probably has to do with his own personality. He tended to take himself out of the picture and preferred to work in privacy. His building and integrating role in the group was considerable. His wife Marion called him the heart of the group. From him Helmuth and I learned to understand and respect conservative living, for during it all he was charitable and had great tolerance. The restless insistence that Helmuth brought to this work complemented Yorck's strengths. Eugen Gerstenmaier aptly describes their different roles with these words: "Perhaps Helmuth Moltke wanted a new society. Peter Yorck was driven by the simple principle of social justice."

It is well known that from the beginning it was important to Helmuth and Peter to bring together a widely diverse group of opponents to the regime. They did this so that as many as possible of the various opponents to the Nazis might have a say. Social Democrats absolutely had to be present, and a connection to labor union leaders had to be found so that workers were represented in the discussions. They succeeded in winning over Adolf Reichwein, who was a Social Democrat. In the late twenties in Silesia, Reichwein had been—like Helmuth and Peter and several others who joined the group—a member of the Löwenberg Arbeitslager, a work camp for workers, students, and farmers. This camp had been established by Helmuth, Carl Dietrich von Trotha, and Horst von Einsiedel, who were students in Breslau at that time, and had been inspired by their teacher Eugen Rosenstock-Huessy. Its goal was to deal with the poverty of the workers in the Waldenburg coal mines. *Arbeitslager* was at that time the innocent term for an innocent activity. Now one understands by the term *Arbeitslager* the terrible camps of the Nazis, and the innocent ones have to be called by the English term *work camps*—also in Germany.

Reichwein won over Carlo Mierendorff and Theodor Haubach to the group; both were Social Democrat Party representatives in the Reichstag until 1933 and then spent a long time in concentration camps. There was also a connection to Wilhelm Leuschner, a former well-known labor union leader. Tasks were assigned that dealt with individual questions within the larger topic: how can a new German democracy work? How can one make democrats out of the Germans? Why did

the Weimar Republic come to such a bad end? The building of the
Reich, the economy, the schools and universities, the punishment of war
criminals, and reparations. How can Europe grow together? All of this
was discussed from 1940 to 1943. Members with differing ideas met in
groups of two, three, or four. There was by no means always agreement.
The representation of different points of view and the compromises that
this logically entailed characterize the work method of the Kreisauers
and belong to the essence of democracy.

Most of these frequent discussions from 1940 to 1943 took place in
Berlin at the Yorcks' on Hortensienstrasse. Marion Yorck was always
there and provided food. Maria Krause, another wonderful Silesian
woman, helped her. "Mariechen" spent almost all of her life in friendship
and loyalty to Peter and Marion, and later, after the execution of Peter
Yorck, she stayed by Marion's side. However, many of the discussions
also took place at Helmuth's small apartment above the garage at 10
Derfflingerstrasse. Kreisau supplied the food for these meetings, so
Helmuth was also able to provide food to his friends in the discussions,
which was an especially pleasant bonus during the war.

I must also report here that we went strictly by the rules for food
rationing. The rules for "self-providers" applied to us. We could not
afford to give easy cause for criticism or persecution due to violation of
necessary rules. Things were certainly not sumptuous for us, but there
were plenty of potatoes, nice vegetables, fruit, flour, and eggs. There
were limited amounts of milk, butter, and poultry, and there was one
fat pig per year.

I was never completely able to get used to east German pig butchering! The pig that had been killed on the farm was brought into our
cellar, and a butcher came to our house in order to cut it up and process
it. A countrywoman was required to knowledgeably and wisely divide
the parts of this animal into meat, sausage, ham, bacon, and lard so
that it could be stretched over a whole year or even longer. It helped
that Mamsell had firm opinions in these matters. Sausage and boiled
pork were cooked in big laundry pots, and carved up meat was lying
spread out on long boards. The whole thing was considered a kind of
folk festival with boiled pork and sausage to eat!

As to the discussions in Berlin, there arose in time the need among the participants to forge an agreement in a more peaceful setting and in a somewhat larger group. They also wanted to write down what they had decided so that it could be discussed by representatives of existing groups or by former members of political groups that had been crushed by the Nazis. Then the consensus could be expanded or changes worked out. Larger meetings would have attracted too much attention in Berlin.

From what has been said so far it is clear that country households were much better suited for this purpose. Besides Kreisau, one meeting, concerning economic questions, was held at Klein Öls, the large Silesian estate of the Yorck von Wartenburg family, and two meetings, concerning agricultural questions, were held at Ernst Borsig's in Groß Behnitz in the Mark Brandenburg. The number of participants at these country meetings was not large. The meetings were basically only an extension of the encounters that continually took place in Berlin. Some very active participants never came to Kreisau: for example, Carlo Mierendorff, who was always very closely watched after his release from the concentration camp, never risked it. He was represented in Kreisau by Haubach. There was also Hans Bernd von Haeften, who felt himself to be represented there by Adam von Trott—both were in the Foreign Service.

That's how the meetings in Kreisau came about. There were only three, but these three long weekends gave us the name "Kreisau Circle," even though the main work was accomplished in Berlin and 50 Hortensienstrasse can be more readily described as the center than Kreisau. However, the whole thing was actually always a loose, informal, nameless group. Probably one of our members—Theo Haubach— used the name "Kreisau Circle" for the first time in an interrogation after 20 July 1944. After that the Security Office (SD) of the SS, which was in charge of the interrogations, took up the name. The SD found very descriptive names for the different resistance groups. For example, they called the circle around Gördeler "Baroque" because older people belonged to it. "Red Band" was the group around Harnack and Schulze-Boysen—its members were mostly, but not exclusively, Communist.

Helmuth probably never heard the name "Kreisau Circle." To my surprise, I heard the name for the first time from the mouth of a civil servant in the justice department, when I, accompanied by Carl Dietrich von Trotha, handed in a plea for clemency after Helmuth's sentencing. Our resistance group surely earned a name of its own. Furthermore, it does not seem inappropriate to me that Kreisau gave its name to the group, for the main motivating force, the actual motor of the whole thing, was the man from Kreisau. And all the members of the group felt that the Kreisau meetings, with their conclusive work, had been especially meaningful.

The German armies had attacked Russia in the summer of 1941. As a result, Helmuth no longer had any illusions about the future of the eastern part of Germany. Whenever I was reticent with a nice jar of jam or some sausage, Helmuth would say, "Aha! You want to save that for Mr. Serpuchov!" That was the imaginary Russian, who would then own Kreisau. Also in the fall of 1941 we invited the painter Karl Schmitt-Rottluff, with whom we were acquainted, and asked him to paint Kreisau. Helmuth thought that the pictures would perhaps remain as a reminder of the place. This was in fact the case—we still have many of these watercolors, strong pictures of a gentle landscape.

The first weekend at Kreisau took place on Pentecost 1942 from 22 to 25 May. The cover story was that Helmuth was inviting his coworkers for a long weekend. They all came by rail but not on the same train. Some of our visitors got off directly in Kreisau, and we met them with a small handcart for their luggage. On Friday evening a full taxi came with the ones who had taken the express train to Schweidnitz, the fastest daytime connection from Berlin. And this occurred again on the two other Kreisau weekends. Besides Helmuth and Peter—with Marion and his sister, the physician Dr. Irene Yorck, called Muto—came Adolf Reichwein, Theodor Steltzer, Harald Poelchau, Hans Peters, and Father Augustin Rösch.

Our house was full of children. Our second son, Konrad, was born in September 1941. In addition, my brother's two children were visiting, and the son of friends from the Rhineland, where bombs were already falling, was always with us. There were also the women: Marion, Muto, Asta, and I. So the whole thing looked like a normal grand hospitable weekend. Perhaps it was also a lucky coincidence for this first meeting in Kreisau that my sister-in-law Asta was to marry in Kreisau exactly one week later. This was known and thus comings and goings were to be expected. None of the Kreisau meetings were purely working meetings. In between sessions we took the nicest walks, and on Sundays some of us walked to Gräditz, where each person could go to his own church.

There was a totally relaxed atmosphere on this first weekend in Kreisau. We also laughed a lot. Today I immediately think of Harald Poelchau, who, as the chaplain in Tegel prison, assisted political prisoners day in and day out and accompanied many of them up to their execution. Yet he was cheerful, I'd like to say a Mozart-type man. Not only did he help political prisoners, but he also helped feed Jews who were in hiding in Berlin. At any rate, several times we sent him sacks of dried peas that had been raised on our farm, which he then distributed. And then there was Father Rösch! I can still see him before me, how he cheerfully told us how to act during a Gestapo interrogation—how one could, so to speak, play a trick on them, although one had to have a guardian angel. Good food also played a role; of course this was due to living in wartime. The food required careful planning beforehand. I remember that my guests loved our Silesian poppy seed stollen. After each of the three weekends I heard how good it was.

The fact that our Kreisau remained such a peaceful island for so long raises the important question of whether we were at all justified in living so peacefully in such times. It's true, the peace at Kreisau was a prerequisite for the genuine and tireless efforts which Helmuth put forth all those years. I approved of and supported Helmuth's efforts and in doing so won for myself a certain inner freedom. Furthermore, we produced necessary food for the general public. However, it required a certain amount of sticking my head in the sand, which I did, for it was unbearable to imagine what was going on. And I protected myself. "Don't look around and just do your work," was basically Helmuth's advice to me. And so I can understand the behavior of the many Germans who did not want to know what was happening in their names, and could not bear to look on. They preferred to know nothing, and in the end even fooled themselves into believing that they knew nothing. But that doesn't excuse us.

In the Berghaus, where we met, we only had room for the Yorcks to stay overnight. I think we also kept Father Rösch with us. He seemed to us to be a very praiseworthy person. As young people we were very proud that the Provincial of the Jesuits, the highest official of the southern German province, took the trouble to visit us. The other four men were housed with our widowed aunts down in the manor. They also ate breakfast there and came up to join us afterward.

Although the Berghaus looked very modest from the outside, it had several comfortable large living areas on the first floor, and high-ceilinged rooms. On the second floor there were many relatively small rooms and the same in the attic. We met in the living rooms and ate all main meals in the dining room of the Berghaus. Helmuth had given strict instructions that there was to be no political discussion during the meals. I had help with the children, and two young women from the village cooked and served for us—Mamsell had unfortunately died already in 1939. Marion, Muto, Asta, and I were always there; we followed everything that was going on but limited ourselves to listening during the meetings. But Marion and I were well informed through our close contact to Peter and Helmuth. Later, after everything was over, including the failed coup on 20 July 1944, and the course of events was already clear for us, one of the two helpers denounced us because of our weekend meetings. If these meetings resulted in more German soldiers having to die, as she assumed, then it was right that she reported them.

There were definite topics for each of the three weekends in Kreisau. For each topic there were discussion leaders. They were well prepared each time. Relatively harmless topics had been chosen for the first weekend; had word about the meetings gotten out, they could have been justified without becoming a matter of treason. The topics were schools and universities, and the relationship between church and state. In fact the participants thought that both topics were centrally important. As concerns the schools and universities, that needs no explanation in view of the destructive effect of the Nazi regime. Adolf Reichwein reported on schools. He had trained teachers until his dismissal and was then a village teacher for six years in Tiefensee near Berlin; now he was working in the Museum of Anthropology in Berlin. Although the group was clearly for the separation of church and state, and there was also agreement in Kreisau about the school plans, in the larger group of Catholics many wanted to retain sectarian elementary schools.

Helmuth then spoke on a reform of the universities. This was also an important question in view of the almost total failure of the universities to be a stronghold against the Nazi state. The topics were discussed, and then two of those present formulated the results reached each time. These summaries were then submitted to the whole Circle, discussed again, and voted on. Steltzer, the oldest of us, a Landrat in Schleswig-Holstein before his dismissal in 1933, led the discussion on church and state. Peters, a professor of public law in Berlin but now drafted into the service, spoke about the concordat that Hitler had concluded with the Catholic Church in 1933. He and Rösch spoke as Catholics, Steltzer and Poelchau as Protestants.

This was also an important topic for various reasons. It's noteworthy that serious Catholics and serious Protestants, representatives of the two large churches that had been split since the Reformation in Germany, sat down at our house and tackled these questions together. Of course, their mutual deep opposition to the Nazi regime, which united them, was a factor. Also there had always been a deep chasm between the churches and the socialists. The churches had failed with regard to the Industrial Revolution. It was Poelchau who believed that the churches ought to concern themselves with social reforms, instead of turning people away just because they were socialists. He always had close contact with workers.

However, questions of faith were also, or became, personally vital for almost all the members of the group. Even if they were not church-going Christians, it was their faith in divine work, and, in fact, the faith rooted in Christian heritage, that gave them their foundation and their courage. Their faith also imposed upon them the duty to act against the destruction of fundamental humanity (evolved from Christianity) by National Socialism and to risk their lives for this. However, for them it was not only a matter of a great heritage, out of which our western treasures had grown, in spite of all atrocities committed by the church and by Christians throughout the centuries; rather, they also believed in the future of Christianity. Christianity has a way— just when it appears bankrupt—of becoming alive again in a new and different manner. They believed that. Faith is tested by one's actions. People attach themselves to many gods and are always in danger of being led astray by false gods—as was the case then with the false gods of National Socialism.

That was the first of the Kreisau weekends. I also remember that on Sunday afternoon my older son, who was five years old, had played "windmill" with an upside down children's bike and had maneuvered his index finger into one of the turning wheels. The tip of the finger appeared to me to be almost off. Quickly to Sister Ida! She believed that if we bandaged it firmly, it would heal. And so it happened; today you can still see something of the injury, but not much.

Many discussions about the results of the first weekend and preparatory work for the second took place mainly in Berlin, but also in Munich and Stuttgart, before the second Kreisau weekend on 16–18 October 1942. This is clearly expressed in Helmuth's letters to me from that summer. In these daily letters, which I wrote to him from Kreisau and he wrote back to me, there was an astonishing amount about the activities of the Friends. We were able to get away with that. Our post office consisted of a woman and her son, the letter carrier, both from Kreisau. The letters from Berlin always reached me in one or two days. That remained so until the end. This was also true for my letters to Berlin, which were completely harmless anyway.

This time, in addition to the key people Yorck and Moltke, the economic expert Einsiedel—who also stood in for the Trothas—came to Kreisau, as well as Haubach, Steltzer, and Peters. New to the second meeting were the theologian Eugen Gerstenmaier from Württemberg and the Jesuit Father Alfred Delp, sent by Rösch from Munich. The labor unionist Leuschner had delegated Hermann Maass, a former socialist youth leader, to join the Circle. However, Maass cannot be called a member of the Kreisauers. He would not have liked that at all. He was always distrustful of the group, above all distrustful of the motives of the participants from noble families. Of the women, Asta was not there. Her husband, Wend Wendland, also a dedicated opponent of the Nazis, now a soldier who fought against becoming an officer in Hitler's army, had asked her not to listen in anymore. He thought it was too dangerous, and there was not much she could do anyway besides listen.

Two meetings were originally planned in the country for the fall, one at the end of September in Klein Öls at the Yorcks' and one at the end of October in Kreisau. The former was for planning for a new state, the latter for economic planning. But Peter and Helmuth thought that holding two meetings so close together was too dangerous, so they combined the two topics for Kreisau. This proved to be too much for one weekend, especially since Helmuth was not completely satisfied with the preparation.

The second Kreisau weekend was not as relaxed as the first. The work went late into the night. For the reconstruction process of both the state and the economy, the ideas of decentralization and self-government were very important for the Kreisauers. They did not propose a return to Baron von Stein's ideas but rather intended to make better democrats out of the Germans by practicing self-government in a more manageable unit. And they wanted to avoid the mistakes of the Weimar Republic. They also wanted to install self-government into the economic sector in the form of so-called company labor unions. A company is described in the Kreisau declarations as a "community of people who work in it," and all members of the company should participate in its decision-making process. The Kreisauers strove for a new, more just social order. These were questions that especially interested Father Delp, who was full of life and ideas. However, it contradicted the hierarchical structure of the labor unions, to which Leuschner wanted to adhere. He was for a large unified labor union, and Maass in Kreisau also leaned in that direction.

Einsiedel and the Trothas had done the groundwork for the questions of economic planning and had provided a basis for discussion. The document that contains the resolutions based on their preparatory work says that the European economy "should be freed from the inherited limitations of a nation-state" in order to "bring about the joining of the separate national economies of Europe into an organic and structured unity." The Kreisauers thought without exception in terms of Europe. Today that almost goes without saying; at that time it was new. They were also all convinced that the sovereign European nation-state was coming to its end in this Second World War; securing world peace required "the creation of an order that comprised the individual states."

There was little time. New wordings were suggested. We always handled written things very carefully. There were only a few copies of everything, and these were carefully guarded. At the Kreisau meetings a typed copy was used as the basis for discussion for each topic that represented the conclusions of the various smaller meetings in Berlin. They then worked together on such copies and made changes. In this way at the second Kreisau meeting they again worked on the declaration of principle, which had originated earlier in the spring. Most of the typed copies were done over the years by Helmuth's secretary in Berlin, Katharina Breslauer, who knew exactly what she was doing.

However, we still took walks as well. That was simply part of the experience. But this weekend was not as cheerful as the first one. There was too much pressure for that. Although they weren't completely finished, in the end Helmuth was satisfied with what had been achieved and especially with the contribution of the new members. These new members were in turn impressed with what had been accomplished in Kreisau.

The third weekend in Kreisau, Pentecost, 12–14 June 1943, had yet another completely different atmosphere. Of course, that was once again strongly influenced by the participants but also by the general conditions. This time there was more pressure from the outside because of the continuing war and the terrible news about the acts of the Germans. All of that prevented what should have been a Pentecost weekend mood. However, I no longer remember whether we spoke much on this weekend about the horrible crimes that were in full swing against Jews above all but also against Russians and Poles.

Besides Yorck and Moltke, Reichwein, Gerstenmaier, Delp, Einsiedel, and Trott attended this meeting. Paulus van Husen, a state-employed lawyer, also attended as a new member. Once again the program was very extensive. The topics were foreign relations questions and how to deal with Nazi and war crimes after the collapse of the Nazi dictatorship, that is, the punishment of the so-called Rechtsschänder—violators of the law.

Trott spoke about foreign policy. Would the West, which at this point was already insisting on unconditional surrender, even listen to Germans? What would the Russians say about it? The German debacle at Stalingrad had already occurred. The foreign policy of the Circle had always consisted of making an attempt to contact anti-German resistance groups in the occupied countries. The Kreisauers believed that would be useful for the time after the war, since representatives of the resistance against the Nazis in Europe, with whom they could work together, would then come to power. They were successful in making contact with the resistance in Holland and Norway but not in France, although Carlo Schmid, whose mother was French, worked toward this end. He was stationed in Lille with the German military government.

Several times Trott had brought news of the existence and the composition of a German opposition to the National Socialists in Germany to Switzerland and Sweden, both neutral countries. Helmuth had done the same. He too went to Sweden, Norway, Denmark, and finally to neutral Turkey. In that way leaflets from the brother and sister Scholl and their friends went through Helmuth to Sweden and from there to England. But there was never a response from England or from the United States.

Husen brought along a draft concerning the "Punishment of the Violators of the Law," which was discussed. The Kreisauers wanted the Germans to be able to participate in the prosecution and sentencing of war and Nazi crimes. They suggested proceedings before an international court, on which the victors, the neutral countries, and Germany would sit together. Sentencing by the victors is seldom recognized by the defeated. Later, though, the Nuremberg trials did become for the Germans an irrefutable and shocking basis for their learning about German war and Nazi crimes.

It was Pentecost. An aunt related by marriage to the Moltkes wanted to visit us in the afternoon. She lived in Schweidnitz where her husband was a judge, but during the war, he was in the East as a reserve officer. We did not refuse her. It would have been conspicuous with the usual comings and goings that were normal with us, for she had established rights. She was the only National Socialist in our family; we always said it was owing to stupidity. So she came in the afternoon. But she was not so stupid that she didn't notice that the meeting of "Helmuth's colleagues" was peculiar. She went for a walk with us. Strangely enough it was Adam Trott, so impressively tall and handsome, whom she didn't trust. And of course she also knew the opinions of her nephew Helmuth

James. She let me know what she thought about this, but I was sure that she wouldn't do anything about it. And so it was. National Socialism didn't go to the point of denunciation with her, for she was a good and loyal person.

So that was the third and final Kreisau weekend. I am not a gifted person when it comes to future premonitions. However, on this weekend, which I found on the whole to be very productive, I suddenly thought—and I can still recall where I was in the house when it came upon me—"This will not go any further."

But it did continue to go quite a while longer in Berlin. On 17 June Helmuth wrote me, "I was at home at 1:30 where Eugen was already waiting and Adam & Haeften also came too late. I had already noticed that the 4 days were perfect bliss for Husen, and that was also the case for Adam & Eugen. Of course that made me very happy, for this bliss is in many respects more important than the concrete result. But there was also general satisfaction with the result, especially with Haeften, who was very impressed."

In August the formulation of the plans was once again altered in some respects during another larger meeting in Berlin, and everything was finally concluded. The final date on the documents was 9 August 1943. The "Principles for the New Order" were combined with the "Directions to the Regional Commissioners." Regional commissioners were supposed to be people who were ready to maintain inner unity on the basis of the Kreisau resolutions in the individual parts of Germany in the event of a collapse, and to act against disintegration.

Included in the directions was naturally the abolition of all discrimination on the basis of race or religion. This demand was already in the first document of principles written down by the Kreisauers and then again in the "Directions to the Regional Commissioners." Helmuth's views toward discrimination and persecution—the way the German atrocities weighed on him all through the rule of the National Socialists—emerge quite clearly from his letters from this time. And he knew that on this matter he was in agreement with his friends in the group.

Regional commissioners were then carefully sought in all of Germany, and some people were found who were ready to take on this responsibility on "Day X," the day on which, defeated from either the inside or the outside, the Third Reich would collapse.

I received a complete copy of the documents and of all papers that Helmuth wanted to save, in order to hide them in Kreisau. Helmuth did not want to know where I hid them. I hid them in an attic of the manor and didn't retrieve them until May 1945, when the Russians occupied Kreisau and set up shop in the big house. I took them with me to the Berghaus and then away with us when we had to leave Kreisau.

Nothing was realized of the plans. Some later resolutions are related to corresponding Kreisau suggestions, but there is no direct connection. First of all, all decisions were made by the victorious allies. They were the ones who once again introduced democracy into the Federal Republic. Also, the Kreisau plans were only intended for "Day X" and for "Zero Hour." The regional commissioners were supposed to be able to prove that in spite of the terror in Germany there were organized opponents to the Nazis, ready for action, who would be able to meet the end with well-thought-out order. The principles, the new starting points, and the orientation were important for them for later, not the details. Those were only recommendations. But one has to give the Kreisauers credit for having asked all the right questions for the future. All their questions needed new answers. Nations are occupied with many of these questions even today. However, many details of the Kreisau recommendations appear strange to a critical eye of today and are no longer comprehensible—for example, everything that has to do with elections. A lot can be understood only in the context of the times and the current situation. Behind the plans stands the participants' great principle protest against a terrorist, criminal dictatorship that despised people to the point of destroying them. The Kreisauers felt duty-bound to act against this dictatorship. It is also a fact that we lived to a certain extent under the illusion, in view of the horrible atrocities of the Third Reich, that with the end of the Nazi regime a stop could forever be put to bondage, oppression, and bloody terror, not only in Germany but in the rest of the world.

Clouds gathered over our Kreisau the following fall. There were many misfortunes in the near and distant family. Of course the war had left its mark on us too. Helmuth's youngest brother, Carl Bernd, had already crashed in an observation plane the year before and was missing, presumed dead. Shortly before the beginning of the war and under difficult circumstances, Willo had cleared out and gone to the United States with all our blessings. "One of us must survive," Helmuth had said. Willo then spent a successful and useful life as an architect in the United States. Jowo [Joachim Wolfgang], the art historian, was a lieutenant in the reserve and during the war was assigned to headquarters in the West as well as in the East, but shortly before Helmuth's arrest he had gone to Norway with Helmuth's help. In this way he also survived, just as we women did.

The time of the heavy bombing attacks on Berlin now began. Many people and administrative authorities left Berlin. There were numerous casualties. The manor in Kreisau filled to the rafters. Only the very big rooms remained empty. We made the most of every corner. In October the Reichwein family, who had lost everything in Berlin owing to the bombing, moved in high up under the roof—the tireless Romai with her four children. They got used to it astonishingly well under the arduous conditions and became true Kreisauers. We were once again a large community of women and children—very different but all working well together. To those who were children then, this community actually remains a pleasant memory.

There was great unrest within the opposition. Many were of the opinion that something absolutely had to happen. Waiting for the victory of the Allies was not enough. One of the most restless was Carlo Mierendorff, a lively, enterprising man with whom Helmuth always especially easily agreed. He was killed by a bomb in November while on a business trip in Leipzig. That was a hard blow for the Kreisauers! Leuschner completely followed the Gördeler group. He was always called "the uncle" in Helmuth's letters to me. On the other hand, the strongest man among the Social Democrats, Julius Leber, grew closer to us. In the letters he was called the "substitute uncle" and also "Neumann." However, Leber always had reservations about the way the Kreisauers theorized too much. I only saw him once at the Yorcks' and never forgot the strong impression he made. He was from Alsace and had opted for Germany after the First World War because he wanted to participate in the very important process of Germany's democratization.

At the Yorcks' Leber also met Colonel Claus Stauffenberg, a cousin of Peter Yorck's. It meant a great deal to Stauffenberg to work with Leber. From this meeting emerged the historically meaningful connection that led to the government coup attempt of 20 July 1944. Helmuth had always felt that the chances of success for a coup were slim. He did not trust the people who could have carried it out. He considered the generals hopeless—even the ones who hated Hitler and his regime, and he also believed that Hitler had to destroy himself. Otherwise he feared that a new "stab-in-the-back" legend would arise. It was one of Hitler's biggest and most successful lies that the Germans did not lose the First World War on the front but lost it because of the unconquered German armies being stabbed in the back by the politicians in Berlin.

Helmuth was still traveling a lot in these months. He too was restless. He had the feeling he did not have much time left. By the end of the year he had been in Brussels, Paris, The Hague, Oslo, Stockholm, Copenhagen, and twice in Istanbul. As always on these trips, he connected his two professions—that of his office with the High Command of the Armed Forces and that of the conspiracy. In his office he dealt with matters important to counterintelligence relative to all foreign countries. For example, in the framework of his office duties he tried—not unsuccessfully—in one of his personal campaigns, which lasted many years, to convince the German occupying armies to stop shooting hostages. He used the argument that the killing of uninvolved, innocent people could only have negative consequences politically for the Germans. Several times he negotiated this topic with the heads of the high commands in the West and with the Security Service of the ss. At any rate, even more innocent people would have died in the West without him. In his conspiracy profession he tried to connect with resistance groups in various countries, and from the neutral countries, he tried to connect with people he knew who were with the Allies. Thus, while in Turkey, he tried to dissuade the Allies from the demand of unconditional surrender on the part of the Germans. But that was unattainable. He returned from his second trip to Istanbul very despondent.

He met Claus Stauffenberg for the first time in December at Peter and Marion's. At Christmas he came to Kreisau for a short visit. We had a sad Christmas celebration. Asta's first, recently born child had died, and our older son was in a hospital in Breslau with a viral lung infection.

Helmuth was arrested on 19 January 1944 in Berlin. It had nothing to do with the Kreisau Circle. He had warned an acquaintance, who had the habit of freely speaking out against the Nazi regime, that he was about to be arrested. Helmuth's warning was discovered, and for that reason he was taken into custody. After some weeks in the notorious basement of Prinz-Albrecht-Strasse, the headquarters of the Gestapo, he went to a small prison that belonged to the women's concentration camp Ravensbrück near Fürstenberg in Mecklenburg. He was only in "protective custody." That meant he had easier and better-than-usual prison conditions. He could read, write, and even continue to work for the OKW. We were able to supply him with extra food. He wore his own clothes. He had a lamp and a teapot.

I had to request permission to speak to him in Berlin at the Gestapo, more precisely at the SD (the Security Service of the SS). For the first time I had to deal with real National Socialists. They always behaved politely toward me. On the basis that I needed his advice in matters having to do with the Kreisau farm, I could visit him once a month. I brought papers from the Kreisau operations with me, and we were allowed to meet at a separate place, the police academy in Drögen. He was brought there by car. I came by train to Drögen, and it was not far from the station by foot. We sat at a corner table in a barracks in the same room with a Gestapo official at a desk. Quite astonishingly, he left us in peace, and he made tea for me. Helmuth had brought the tea and the pot from his cell. We probably had about two hours together, and our conversations were not monitored, so we were able to speak freely. We were also allowed to write each other—he, every three to four days, and I must have written every day. Everything was read, and apparently my letters were read with enjoyment. In any case I was once told by the official who sat at the desk how sorry he was that I had such bad luck with my geese. I commented afterward to Helmuth that these were really quite friendly people. "Except that they rip your nails out during interrogations," he replied. But that—or anything similar—never happened to him.

Kreisau continued to play a big role for Helmuth in the months of his imprisonment until the end of his life. Kreisau—thoughts of the beautiful country in every detail, of the farm, but above all, of us, his closest family that he knew was still living there in peace. All of that made him feel stronger and gave him comfort. Thinking of Kreisau only brought him joy, not worries. In the beginning of July they talked of releasing him, not back to his office but as a worker in an ammunition factory.

I spent the night at the Yorcks' in Berlin on each of my trips. Marion was now more often in Silesia because of the many bombs that were falling on Berlin. Sometimes both of them were there, sometimes only Peter. It felt like entering an oasis when I came to them and was warmly taken in. I remember once when I arrived late in the evening, coming from Drögen after a trip through the rubble of Berlin, how Peter went down to the cellar and fortified me with a bottle of rare, wonderful wine which he had been able to save.

But then came the coup attempt, on 20 July 1944. The assassination attempt on Hitler failed, as well as the coup. After the extensive arrests and interrogations, it quickly came out that Helmuth belonged to the active opposition. Several days earlier, in the first few days of August, I had again received permission to speak to him. Helmuth was fully aware of the danger of his situation and even the situation in general. I believe it was the day on which Peter Yorck had been sentenced to death by the Freisler court and had been executed immediately. Before his execution in Plötzensee, at the place of execution, Peter told Harald Poelchau, who, as the prison chaplain, was allowed to enter, that nothing was revealed in the interrogations about the work of the Kreisauers. But a few days later that also came out. During our last meeting Helmuth had already arranged with me that he would let me know his situation by writing to me whether a certain forty-acre-large paddock in Kreisau should be completely plowed up. If so, that meant his situation was hopeless; if he only indicated a part of it, this would then describe his chances.

I knew that his situation had become serious because only short messages were arriving. Only ten lines were allowed and these only seldom. In one of these communications it said that three-quarters of the forty acres in Kreisau should be plowed up. After that the messages stopped coming.

So at the end of September I decided to travel to Drögen without a permit to find something out. I was greeted in a friendly way at the police academy. "Oh, it's good that you've come. Your husband was transferred to Berlin yesterday and here are all his things. He also needs a suit." I asked where Helmuth had gone. They said to the ss prison on Lehrter Strasse. While I dragged the heavy suitcase with Helmuth's things to the train station, it became clear to me what the situation was. Then on the train back to Berlin who should come into my compartment but the Gestapo man who had always treated me in a friendly manner. In the course of our sparse conversation I asked him, wanting to hope again, whether things were bad. He said, "Yes, very bad!"

In Berlin I immediately went to the Lehrter Strasse prison. Helmuth was no longer there because the jail had just sustained heavy bombing damage. "Oh, the tall man," the ss man on guard said. "He went to Tegel." To hear that made me very happy for a moment. Tegel was Harald Poelchau's prison. That meant there was a possibility of connecting with Helmuth.

And indeed that's how it was. For almost four months until Helmuth's death we could write each other daily. For four months Harald and Dorothee Poelchau surrounded Helmuth and me with their inexhaustible friendship, at risk to themselves. And until the end of Helmuth's life Harald managed to smuggle in his pockets foodstuff from Kreisau into Helmuth's cell. Besides Helmuth, Eugen Gerstenmaier and Alfred Delp from the Kreisau community were also imprisoned at Tegel at that time. They were also taken care of by the Poelchaus. Many of our women were in Moabit prison; however, after several months they were all released. At the time of Helmuth's death Marion Yorck was free again. Poelchau's duties as chaplain extended also to Moabit prison, so he was able to stand by our women; and he brought them honey rolls as well. So there was a lot of interaction with the outside, as is usually the case in most prisons, but above all at that time in prisons that were run by the judicial authorities such as Tegel and Moabit rather than the ss. But even in the ss prisons there were helpful people.

I was probably not arrested because I was already well known to the Gestapo. I was mostly in Berlin during these months, for we were expecting Helmuth's trial at any time; however, to our relief, which was continually renewed, it was delayed several times. I always went only for short trips to Kreisau mainly to get food; only over Christmas was I there for a longer time. Asta, who after her marriage had at times lived elsewhere, was now back at Kreisau. She shouldered the burden of everything with us. Indeed, all of Kreisau gave us enormous support during these months.

In Berlin I stayed with Carl Dietrich von Trotha, Helmuth's cousin. Peter Yorck was dead, Marion was still in jail, and an ss family was living in her house. Trotha's family had also left Berlin because of the bombing danger. It was courageous of Carl Dietrich, whose membership in the Kreisauers was never discovered, to let me stay in his home, and I was very thankful. Because of Helmuth I now had the honor of being a "leprous" person.

Brigitte Gerstenmaier had also remained free. She was also in Berlin, and we shared the troubles and uncertainty of the times. She enjoyed the friendship of the Poelchaus as well. Almost daily we picked up messages and received consolation from them in their apartment in Wedding on Afrikanische Strasse, exchanged letters, and restored our strength. We often traveled together in the subway and city train from the Poelchaus' on one end of Berlin to our respective lodgings at the other end of the city that was burning above us. Such an experience establishes a lifelong friendship!

Finally on 10 and 11 January 1945 the trial took place before the People's Court. Helmuth, Delp, and Haubach were sentenced to death but were not executed directly following the trial. Gerstenmaier came away with a prison sentence. All of them went back to Tegel again. Helmuth was executed on 23 January 1945.

The Last Months in Kreisau

Marion Yorck and I traveled from Berlin to Kreisau on 25 January 1945. Edith and Henssel took us to the train. They had the nicest sandwiches for us, and Marion had a bottle of very old Malaga. The bottle was wrapped in paper or in a napkin; it looked as though it were coffee with milk. Marion and I sat closely together on a little two-seater bench in third class. We were traveling against the flood of refugees and so it took exactly twenty-four hours to get to Kreisau, but in my memory it was a good trip. I think we were quite cheerful. No one in Kreisau knew yet about Helmuth's death. Wend was there with Asta, and eight or nine soldiers, a whole antiaircraft unit, had come with him. Frau Pick, Helmuth's former housekeeper in Berlin, was happy to be busy cooking for all these men. Ulla Oldenbourg, with her companion, had already been with us for months, and Maria Schanda was also there. Marion traveled immediately on to Nimptsch, where Muto (Irene Yorck) practiced medicine but was currently sick in bed with diphtheria. It was very difficult for me to tell little Caspar about his father. He lay in my bed, where he had slept; I sat on the edge. But we got through it and on the next morning when he saw that I was sad, he asked, "Because of Pa? Still?!" That was really a great comfort.

Everything was a mess. The Russians quickly advanced west. The house, the manor, and the village had been full of [German] refugees from the other side of the Oder [River] for several weeks. In the Berghaus they were staying in the living rooms. Their cart stood unhitched at the house, and the farm below was full of the trekking carts of others.

Something had to be done; everyone was undecided. Looking back, the days seemed to me like weeks until the original manor inhabitants, the children, the Zeumer daughters—both of whom, like Asta, were expecting a child—until Ulla and her companion, and Asta herself departed from Schweidnitz to the West with the hospital train. It must have been in the early days of February. Wend and his "little men," as Frau Pick called them, had already left. His small unit had to protect an especially valuable piece of equipment. This task gave them the marvelous opportunity to clear out again and again. They couldn't stay with us anyway. There was snow on the ground, and we traveled in two sleds to Schweidnitz in order to take the travelers to the hospital train. Asta sat facing the back in the first sled; I sat in the second sled facing the front. I can still see her sad, quiet face. It emerged again and again, filled with silent grief. What would become of all of us? Then the first sled pulled forward and Asta's face disappeared. Ten minutes later we caught up with them, and again her face emerged with the same expression. Then they all departed. Later on, in April, I unexpectedly received a postcard from her, when mail from the West came through once again. She had traveled to the Wendland relatives in Mecklenburg and was now setting out from there to Holstein in order to have her child at Aunt Leno's.

A few days after this group of women and children had started out, Zeumer called me in from the farm to the Berghaus in the early morning: "Now the time has come!" he said. "Our village must trek!" Women, children, and old people were supposed to go to Czechoslovakia by order of the Party. I was determined to remain for the time being. How were we to manage on the roads in the middle of winter? The Russians were not yet here. Also, Helmuth had advised me to stay as long as possible. In Ravensbrück he had discussed our situation through the window with General Halder, who was in the cell next to him. They both felt that our mountain area was safe and believed that the Russians, in their advance toward Berlin, would pay no attention to us since we were on their left flank. Furthermore, the old Countess Yorck and her daughter Do had recently come to stay with me. Romai Reichwein and her children, who were still living in the manor, wanted to stay.

However, on this morning a sad group was forming down on the farm and on the village road. Frau Zeumer went with them. Zeumer, Süßmann—the mayor of the village—and I stood on the farm next to the lines of carts that were forming. We kept only the milk-cart horses and a few young foals—all the other horses were taken along. I can still see our farm people in front of us—Frau Meyer, old Frau Rose, Frau Kaiser, and others. Women with children had already been taken away in the tractor with a trailer. But there was snow on the Eule Mountain passes, the streets were full of refugees, the trailers slid—we dared not fill them too full. The Stäsche family, our odd gardeners who lived next to us on the Berghaus hill, had already left. The invalid Stäsche with his distorted face, who could barely speak and had a bad limp, asserted again and again that he did not want to be "slaughtered."

Sister Ida was still there on this morning with her children. I had convinced her she shouldn't move out with them over hastily. When I went to the village the next morning, she was gone with all her foster children. She had gotten a special car from the army and had taken advantage of this opportunity. She became separated from the Kreisauers, reached Bavaria rather quickly, and on the whole had an easier time of it during this wild period.

The soul of the village was gone with her, however. It hurt every time I went past the empty *Spielschule* in the next few months. How often I, with and without Helmuth, had called on her, had sat in the wicker chairs in her room, and had spoken about the problems of the village. I can still hear Helmuth asking *Schwesterchen* [little sister] how things were going in the village. She knew everything. She influenced the people with love and a lot of common sense, and she ruled the village children, all of whom had been through her school, with a strict hand and a shrill voice. The field marshal had established the *Spielschule*, and it had been supported by the farm until the great economic crisis came. Then it was taken over by the village, and the farm continued to support it but only as the largest taxpayer.

Sister Ida was close to everyone, including the Moltkes. She had come before Jowo was born. She maintained herself and her household with foster children who were assigned to her by the welfare office. When we called on her we usually chatted for quite a while, while the children scratched on the door and wanted to come to "Mamma"—and only with great effort could she keep the children from rushing into the room. One of them was always sitting on her lap anyhow. Everything always lay around in her room in big heaps. "It looks crazy here, doesn't it?" she would say and would wipe the table with her blue deaconess apron; then we'd sit down in the wicker chairs. Now she was gone and the *Spielschule* was empty.

I didn't have much time to think about that, however, because after the departure of our village residents, Davy Moltke arrived almost immediately with the Wernersdorf trek. The town of Wernersdorf had just been taken by the Russians, so they really had to leave. Davy came with her whole entourage—there were even many members of the Yorck household with her. Männa von Berlichingen an aunt of the Yorcks whose presence did our house good, came. The old Mademoiselle of the Mirbachs, a spinster and the cook for the older Countess Yorck, also came, as well as the housekeeper and the private tutor of the family in Wernersdorf. The children were already in Mecklenburg. Just after Davy and her trek arrived, Marion and Muto arrived from Nimptsch. I met them nearby at the Nieder-Gräditz farm. They arrived on foot— a car had dropped them off close by. I was so relieved and happy to see them. They remained in Kreisau. The village was now occupied by German soldiers. They came from Russia and were determined to leave as little as possible behind for the Russians. No one came to the Berghaus—it was too much out of the way and from the distance looked so unprepossessing. But down below on the farm there was a lot of commotion. After another week the Wernersdorf group decided to move on to Glatz County. The older Countess Yorck and Do remained temporarily behind with us, but after Davy was able to settle everyone into Glatz, she fetched her mother, and we were once again alone. I believe that Marion and Muto were already coming and going at that time. The Berghaus was their headquarters. The agonizing indecision concerning the question whether or not to trek plagued us too.

The Russian front was approximately ten kilometers away. The Russians were firing; some days the noise was disturbing and seemed to be coming nearer. Striegau was taken by the Russians; Wernersdorf was Russian. But we were in contact with our German garrison. A major and a lieutenant sat in the Blue House on the street to Gräditz, and a military rationing unit, which provided food for the front, was staying in the manor. Food for the troops on the front was distributed from all our barns. The delegations rushed down the village street in their Russian Panje carts and on their Panje horses and picked up their supplies on the farm. Whole cows, sheep, and pigs hung in the cellar and in the old kitchen of the manor, and there were piles of sausage. Shoes and clothes were stored in the vestibule. The rest of the manor was not occupied out of respect for the name of the old field marshal. The children loved the rationing staff for they had candy. Zeumer was also quite satisfied because the high-ranking officers of the unit were staying with him and fed him superbly. These people were all fat, well fed, and Nazis; they still talked about victory and several days later said they would continue fighting no matter what.

We reburied the field marshal and his wife in Helmuth's and my empty graves. The casket of his sister remained alone in the chapel where all three caskets had lain in the open next to each other. We attempted to lower her casket over Papi's,[1] but it wouldn't go in. Eight sergeants in steel helmets were detailed to carry the caskets down. Schmolke, Süßmann, Zeumer, and I were present, as well as the major and the lieutenant. It was quite ceremonious and at the same time so wretched.

We often went to the Blue House to find out about the military situation and because the connection with the army made us stronger in face of the Party. One day an inhabitant of the Blue House was looking for us and asked whether we wanted to stay or move out. He was determined to stay. He was a longtime opponent of the Nazis and through his daughters had contact with two Russian workers, who in reality were Russian officers and spies. They were stationed in Oberweistritz. He had protective papers from these Russians.

The men who had not already been drafted a long time ago remained in the village. When the front was no longer moving in our direction many of the women came back illegally from Czechoslovakia to Kreisau and stayed a short time or longer. Our people were in a village not far

---

[1] Freya's father-in-law.—*Trans.*

from Prague on the Bohemian plain. Only Poles still worked on the farm.

Romai still lived upstairs in the manor, but she came up to the Berghaus in the evenings in all kinds of weather in order to hear the English news. We tried to prepare for our retreat, should the occasion arise. We stored a load of potatoes, flour, and a couple of suitcases in Michelsdorf in the mountains, near the Weistriz Dam. To do that we had to bicycle far into the mountains. The Eule villages had not yet been evacuated, but the people there were in constant worry about whether they would have to go today, tomorrow, or the day after. We thoroughly enjoyed the beauty of the country during such excursions. The Russians came in individual planes and dropped bombs. The German soldiers called these individual planes "Otto Müllers," which flew in singles like mosquitoes. They mainly attacked the Weizenrodau Airfield. From our place you could see them circle there and drop the bombs. It looked like a game not like serious danger. Yet one morning we—Marion, Muto, and I—came along bicycling happily, as though nothing were wrong, from Ludwigsdorf to Leutmannsdorf, where several bombs had just fallen and several people had been killed. I saw the body of a woman lying on a dung heap near the mill above, and when we came to the pastor, we found a child there, dying of a serious injury to the head. The child seemed beautiful and full of wisdom; he groaned, his mother cried, and the pastor comforted. Marion was deeply affected. We had wanted to ask the pastor for the addresses of people who lived deeper in the mountains, with whom we could find shelter for the six children if necessary.

Frau Pick was very nervous and wanted to leave. After her Berlin experiences she could no longer endure the bombs, and she maintained that she knew exactly which blast stemmed from a gun and which from a bomb. On the one hand she wanted to leave, leave, leave, and when I talked about leaving she wanted to stay, stay, stay. The whole thing passed over the children completely. They played, ate, and slept, and were completely unconcerned. However, looking back, it seems to me that everything also passed over me completely. It went on day after day, but everything was like a dream.

Then came a couple of stern warnings from the Party leadership in

Gräditz, saying that I should leave Kreisau immediately. Finally they demanded that we leave Kreisau within two days or else we would be driven from town to town by the police. I went by bicycle to the Party office in Gräditz. It was located right next to our butcher; earlier Herr Suhr and later a younger butcher had sold us our meat there until both were sentenced to long prison terms because of illegal butchering practices—neither one was a Nazi. The Party office was across from the brick factory in which there had last been a Jewish camp. There was an atmosphere of unrest there, and the local branch leader was not at all happy to see me. The Moltke case was utterly unpleasant to him. He assured me—in a friendly way—that it was completely intolerable to have six children in his district but that Wierischau, the second outlying farm from Kreisau, no longer belonged to his district and so did not concern him. He would gladly give me one more week. So after one week all the children moved with Romai into two rooms of the uninhabited Wierischau farmhouse. That was actually not bad. They lived there very happily and came to see me often in the Berghaus, where we celebrated Easter.

Then I lost my nerve after all and decided to take the children away. A short time earlier Romai had found a small empty farmhouse in Pommerndorf, above Hohenelbe in the Riesen Mountains. It was almost a thousand meters high, but it was situated on the Czech side of the mountains. After Easter we set off for the place. Two box carts full of luggage, six children, old Fräulein Hirsch (the daughter of the forest warden), Aunt Leno's Bertha, Frau Pick, Romai, and I. Our drivers were two Poles. I always had the feeling that all of this was a waste of time, but I didn't have the nerve to stay. I remember that I told Marion and Muto before they left to look for their family in Mecklenburg that I had to "bite into the wrong apple"—and bite we did. We traveled to Michelsdorf on the first day, to Friedland on the second, and to Trautenau on the third. There the children remained with Frau Pick and Romai in the hotel and came the next day by train to Hohenelbe. The living conditions were still normal here. This area behind the mountains, already in Czechoslovakia, had escaped the war in every respect. The trek was beautiful. Spring had come, and the weather was dry and sunny. Our two heavily loaded wagons rolled slowly but surely through the mountains. I remember an especially beautiful place between Friedland and Schömberg, a magnificent mountain pass. The children remained in the inn below and ate potato soup. Fräulein Hirsch and I went ahead with one wagon and four horses. Then the horses turned around and picked up the children and the second wagon, to which a coach had been attached for tired children. We were waiting above in the forest. The hour I spent there is unforgettable. Fräulein Hirsch was sleeping soundly. Across the pass the view opened to the Riesen Mountains. I sat in the heart of the Silesian Mountains and was surrounded by the full beauty of this landscape, a curious mixture of gentleness and austerity in color and form, of great vastness and charming nearness. The children were once again completely unconcerned and enjoyed the whole thing as a fun adventure. We had a difficult time getting the heavy wagons over the mountain above Hohenelbe. The houses—there were about ten of them—stood high up in the mountains in a meadow.

The older children soon went to a school that had a Nazi teacher. However, he was somewhat shocked by the general situation at that point and gladly dealt with our children in a good and friendly way. We further increased our food supplies, for in Bohemia there was still an unlimited amount of food, and we had brought along plenty with us besides.

After three weeks I left the children in order to see about Kreisau. I went by bicycle. Actually, I had only wanted to bicycle to Trautenau, that is, out of the mountains and then about three hours in a northeasterly direction. I continually had the mountains on my left side in all their glory. I traveled through the prosperous rural country in all its spring greenness—it reminded me of Austria. In Trautenau, at one o'clock in the afternoon, I ascertained that the next train did not leave until the following morning. It was still early, and I felt in good shape, so I decided to see how far in the direction of Kreisau I could get. I now knew the way well, and such glorious spring beauty made me extremely happy. When I passed by Friedland around five o'clock, I was gradually getting tired, and Helmuth's bicycle, on which I had always comfortably ridden, became uncomfortable. But I knew that from the top of the Reinsbach valley on—through the so-called Silesian valley—it would then be only downhill. So I continued to ride, and rode and rode; I saw Eule Mountain from behind, then came into its shadow, rode along the long Wüstewaltersdorf valley, turned at Kynau into the Weistritz Dam, and rode along the magnificent Talsperre Road down to Oberweistritz. The day was now slowly beginning to wane, but my joy at soon seeing Mühlberg and the chapel hill on the horizon and my growing anticipation at arriving home again gave me wings. I left the mountains behind me and traveled toward Ludwigsdorf. The chapel hill appeared with its spruces, Mühlberg with its acacia top, and after I had climbed over the small Ludwigsdorf ridge, there lay before me Wierischau, there lay Kreisau, and the Berghaus with the large acacia tree next to it beckoned. It was wonderful to come home! Muto and Marion had returned from Mecklenburg, had not yet expected me, and joyfully welcomed me. Here was the house, my room, my bed. It was around 7:30; at 9:30 in the morning I had set out—it was probably about a hundred kilometers through the mountains. On this evening I had the feeling that all the happiness and richness of our Kreisau life had come together in me once more during this journey home.

I remained three or four days in Kreisau. I have especially happy memories of these days. Then I left again and returned to the children. That must have been during the last days of April, for the Third Reich was then coming quickly to an end. The Russians were fighting in Berlin. Hitler was locked in the Reich chancellery. We were sitting on our high mountain and tried to obtain news. We did not have a radio. So Romai and I climbed even higher up to the place of the Reichweins' old friend, through whom we had located our little houses. When we arrived there the news was just coming in that the Russians had conquered Berlin. It was thought that Hitler had killed himself in the Reich chancellery. The people up there asked, "Can that be true?" But I knew immediately and with certainty that it was true. The Third Reich was over!

Now the Russians would occupy Kreisau. I believed that it would be necessary to be there at that time. Again I left the children with Romai and Frau Pick. This time Fräulein Hirsch came with me. Again we went by bicycle but stayed overnight on the way. Together with Marion and Muto, I waited in Kreisau for the Russians. The German men were restless. We hadn't had ardent Nazis in the village, but the halfway ones now became nervous. They asked me what they should do. "Stay," I said, but the shopkeeper Franke and mayor Süßmann did leave Kreisau during these last days. However, they returned several weeks later. Zeumer had a good idea. "Now, before it's all completely over, the village trek must be brought back," he said. "Afterward it could be too late." He was worried about his wife. "I shall go there and bring the people back." He left Kreisau and undertook to do that. Even the Poles, who had for years lived with their families in Kreisau and worked on the farm, now became restless. One of them said, "If you stay, we'll also stay."

On one of these days, as I was walking through the village, a motorcycle with a Russian soldier on it came down Kirschallee. Behind him sat a civilian, and a lilac branch in bloom decorated the front of the motorcycle. The soldier stopped when he saw me. The civilian, a Pole as it turned out, asked me in broken German whether the bridge across the Peile was intact; when I said yes, they traveled over the bridge to the train station and back again. A few hours later the Russian army began to roll through Kreisau. It was quite a sight. There were primitive aspects such as wagons loaded high with booty and run down vehicles, but the men exuded vitality and were healthy and strong—in short, they were victorious. A current of vitality was pouring through the small, out-of-the-way village of Kreisau, whose undestroyed bridge had become important.

Marion, Muto, and I did not want to miss this show but soon had to give it up, for the Russian soldiers were chasing all the women. We had been standing there completely in the open in the entrance to the Kreisau farm under the two gladiators on the columns to the left and right, and that was not the wise thing to do. We fled and in the following days learned the art of hiding ourselves. We also did not sleep in the Berghaus but rather in our neighbor's small barn on the Berghaus hill or with old people. We felt for the first and only time quite unsafe in these days. But after the army had marched through, everything calmed down, and after a few days we even dared to go by foot to Schweidnitz. We hoped to get protection against attacks by men from the commanding officer there. We actually did get through to see him and asked if he knew how the Russians all around were behaving.

He did not understand at all what we wanted and only said in a friendly way that every man needed a woman. That's just the way things were.

Even before we went to Schweidnitz, the village trek had indeed returned. Completely safe and sound, with all their horses and possessions, and undisturbed by the Russian army marching in the opposite direction from Kreisau to occupy Czechoslovakia. The Russians had only encouraged them to return to their villages. Zeumer had pressed for a quick departure, had led the convoy on side roads, and crossed the Czech-German border before the Czechs had anything to say about it. The whole village was no longer together, but many farm families and all of our farmwomen were there again.

I was worried about the children and also wanted to bring my small trek back. Zeumer gave me a horse, a light old cart, and an obliging young man to take along. He was a baker and knew as little about horses as I did. He had not become a soldier due to severe rheumatic fever. A Russian had written a note for me: "This woman is on her way to pick up her children and bring them home." There was nothing else on the note, above all, no stamp. I don't even recall if it was signed. Once again I traveled the well-known route over the mountains. I had only two obstacles to overcome, although once again we encountered Russian soldiers streaming back. I remember that a young fellow came up to my cart, rummaged through my backpack, examined and inspected everything, and picked out only a good pocketknife to take with him. The first obstacle was a Pole who came toward us with a gang of men. He wanted my horse. But then it was not good enough for him. He gave the horse a swat and let us continue. The second obstacle was two Russians who stopped us and apparently wanted to know what our plans were. I held out my note to them. The more important of the two men did not like the note, but the less important man talked to him in a friendly manner. I didn't understand anything, but it sounded like "Just let her go on her way." And that he did. In this way I actually came to the children. There I discovered that all the adults were pale. Something truly terrible had happened.

The Germans had put the so-called Wlassov Russians in a camp, over one thousand meters in altitude, in the Riesen Mountains. These were

Russians who were ready to fight against Communism and who were performing drills there. These Russians feared their advancing fellow countrymen, and at the last moment the Germans had dissolved the camp and discharged them with their arms. The most important thing for the Russians was, of course, to get rid of their German uniforms and find civilian clothing. A few days before my return, Renate Reichwein had gone as usual to pick up milk in the morning at the home of a nearby farmer, who was also our landlord. The farm lay quite isolated, separated from our hillside by a strip of forest. Renate arrived to find the kitchen empty and looked for the farmer's wife in the house and the barn. There lay the family of four, murdered. Russians searching for clothing had killed all of them. They had not approached the group of houses in which we lived.

It was shortly before Pentecost. Romai suggested postponing the return trip until after Pentecost, but I did not want to put it off one more day. Again we obtained a note. This time it was written in Czech, by a teacher, and there was more to it. The sense of it was, "These women, whose husbands were sentenced to death and executed by the National Socialist regime, are moving with their children back to their home town of Kreisau in Silesia." And again this note served us well. The trek back was not easy. We took only one cart and the small coach. We left a lot of luggage in the mountains. We had only three horses. They had been kept the whole time at a farmer's in the valley below. They had been well fed, but the cart was piled high with luggage and food under the tarp, and it was difficult for the horses. A wheel on the box cart broke down completely while we were still on the Czech side. The blacksmith whom I fetched made the cart function again—without our having to unload everything—with an old wheel. We had been able to push wooden blocks under the wheel just as it was breaking down. He shook his head in wonder. "What strange people you are!" Obviously not farmers, knew nothing of horses and carts, not a knowledgeable man among them. He was not used to such treks. But the Sudenten Germans were friendly, and we all managed the strain well.

On the first night we slept in the hay at a Sudenten German farmer's. The next morning we arrived at the border. The Czechs there were no longer friendly, but the note worked. They looked at us critically and skeptically, and they took away the third horse we had used as a leader to go up hill. My protest did not help. We were supposed to be happy that they didn't take anything else—they were probably right about that—and we crossed the border. On the right and the left sides of the road, German military vehicles lay in the ditch. In the bushes one could pick up bundles of German cash. We didn't touch anything and just moved on. We made slow progress; on the eve of Pentecost we were at the Grüssau monastery. We stayed there overnight, and on Pentecost we heard High Mass in the large, magnificent Baroque church. The large church was full; it was very festive. Then we continued on our way.

Behind Grüssau, on a hill, when the horses were exhausted, I laid a stone under one of the wheels and the ring finger on my right hand was caught. It was not all that bad, but bad enough that the horses had to pull again in order to free my finger. A short time later our little dog, Flitz, a black Scotch terrier who was always neglected but dearly loved, and who usually came along with us, was run over by a Russian truck. Fräulein Hirsch remained a bit behind with the bicycle and buried the dear animal. But those were our only cases of misfortune, and even today it still seems like a miracle that the five women, six children, and the half-grown man actually arrived in Kreisau in one piece. When I drove down from Ludwigsdorf to Wierischau I was a bit proud that I returned Zeumer's milk-cart team in perfect condition. After Easter, Zeumer had parted with his team for our benefit.

Now the summer began. In the beginning we didn't notice the Russians much. There was only a small occupying force, and they generally left us in peace. At first they wanted to make me the mayor, but I didn't want that. So instead they got a decent Kreisau man, who proved to be very good. We all got back to our work as quickly as possible. We continued to till the fields. We had a limited number of workers; we had our horses, machines, and cows. However, these weren't our own herds; ours had been picked up at the beginning of February by the Party and driven to Waldenburg to the slaughterhouse. Zeumer had protested but was severely threatened and had to let the cattle be taken away. Around the same time a lot of cattle had been simply let loose during the chaos of the evacuation of the villages in Czechoslovakia. They stood bellowing in the meadows because they had not been milked. We couldn't leave them there like that, and soon our beautiful old stable was completely full of this thrown together herd. The animals were still with us when the war ended. Although there were some difficulties, we got things up and running and paid our people with food. We all had enough to eat, and every now and then we butchered a cow for the whole village.

I went by bicycle to Schweidnitz and looked for our former teacher, Fräulein Seiler, the daughter of the local photographer. We took her in with us at the Berghaus and opened the school again. Romai also moved into the Berghaus with her children. We had already cleared out the living rooms below in February for the first group of refugees. The Reichweins took over these rooms. It was easier, with regard to the Russians, to hold onto a house that was full and well used. One day Liesbeth from Striegau also came back. Raised by Sister Ida, she had been our household help and nanny. When we evacuated, she had decided to live with her mother. Now she returned to us. Marion and Muto undertook an extensive reconnaissance by foot to Kauern and Klein Öls, during which they pulled behind them a handcart loaded with their backpacks. Later they were the first ones to leave Silesia after its conquest and to look for their relatives in Mecklenburg. But they always returned to the Berghaus for longer periods.

Everyone was living a relatively well-ordered, industrious life in the village, on the farm, and in the Berghaus. The children were doing wonderfully. The household was running; I was on the farm a lot, in the village and the surroundings, and as before, I drove with Zeumer across the fields. At first the Russians sometimes still tried to come into the house in the evenings, but the door to our house withstood the onslaught. In the evenings we carefully and securely locked all the shutters and doors. However, it was not a pleasant feeling when a Russian rattled on the doors like crazy and jiggled the door handle. But it was known that such actions were not supported by their superiors. If one was able to get help from outside, even from Germans, then the Russians ran away. So I sat upstairs with the fire horn in order to fetch the neighbor Raschke in an emergency—but it never came to that.

The Russians also stole—but in moderation. Once I caught a Russian right in the act. When one confronted them without fear, they were always reasonable, even friendly. Only fear made them wild—that, they couldn't bear at all. The chickens—we only had about fifteen left—were industrious layers and were very valuable to us. They now lived with us at the Berghaus, although previously they had not been allowed there. Following Mami Moltke's practice, I had entrusted them to the care of old Frau Rose on the farm; she invariably kept the newly hatched chicks safe for a few days in her bed. Frau Zeumer despised our inappropriate attitude toward our chickens. This attitude was not proper for a Silesian countrywoman. No doubt many eggs were lost between the farm and the Berghaus, but I was satisfied when Frau Rose appeared every week with a big white enamel bowl full of eggs and drank coffee with Mamsell in the kitchen. Since the chickens, which until recently had numbered a remarkable three score (sixty hens) approximately, had dwindled substantially, the rest were better protected near us. The call "there's a Russian in the hen house!" therefore did not sound pleasant. I still see his happy face before me as he put one hen after the other in a sack. "But don't take all of them," I called anxiously. He laughingly shook his head, showed six with his fingers, and shortly afterward disappeared with his loot.

Defending the bicycles was difficult. The Russians wanted to have them all, but they were very important to us. I caught a Russian as he was taking my last one out of the yard of the Berghaus. I tried to explain to him how important one bicycle was for us. He understood me perfectly well. After a short time actually all the Russians could speak some German. He assured me he would bring the bicycle back in the evening. That was the usual excuse, and everyone knew that it wasn't true. So I laughed, and then he also laughed and let me keep the bicycle.

During the course of the summer the manor was occupied by an entire Russian company. They were supposed to supervise our harvest. Fräulein Hirsch had moved back into the lower level of the manor. During the war years she had lived there with her father, who later died. Old Hirsch had come to Kreisau as a retired forest ranger. In exchange for a free apartment he regularly went through the various shrub areas and kept the chapel hill with the burial chapel of the field marshal in order. The Moltke family tomb was also there. He helped the hunt leaseholders as well. During the years when Helmuth sought to save Kreisau from a compulsory auction, he had leased the hunt to a group of doctors from Schweidnitz, and that remained so until the end. After Hirsch's death, the daughter had kept the downstairs apartment in the manor and along with it, the care of the chapel hill and the field marshal's room.

This room behind the large white-golden dining room had been left unchanged since his death in 1891. Everything was still there—from the pink porcelain stand for his wigs and the small washbasin to the felt slippers and the big black Maltese coat from Moiré in the closet; from the plumed helmet to the Moltke family tree, which covered the whole wall. Pilgrims came by foot to visit the chapel hill, and they wanted to see the room. The modesty of this room made a deep impression on them again and again, especially during the Nazi period. So that was the room of a field marshal! Usually the aunts, when they were living in the manor during the summer and sometimes also during the winter, conducted the guided tour. But when they were not there, the Hirsch family stood in for them. During the war, when the manor was filled to the brim with refugees—families from Berlin who wanted to get out of the way of the bombs—Fräulein Hirsch became a kind of manor housekeeper. She did that enthusiastically and helped me a lot. She was a good soul. She went through thick and thin for us. After the trek she got together with Aunt Leno's famous Bertha below in the manor. Bertha was also a true Silesian, a fine and capable woman. She had her heart in the right place. When Aunt Leno left with her grandchildren in the hospital train, Bertha decided to stay with their belongings and protect them.

When the Russian company moved into the manor, both women found work and sustenance. Fräulein Hirsch helped in the kitchen; Bertha sewed, mainly brassieres. They were in great demand with Russian women—and there were many of them around. I visited Fräulein Hirsch and Bertha every few days and got to hear the latest Russian gossip—what they ate, how much better the captain lived (he got his potatoes fried in pure butter only), the womanizing, what terrible condition the lavatories were in (soon they were given up, and the whole company, including the captain, used two privies outside). The two old women were overwhelmed by all of this, and they also wanted to consult with me. Fräulein Hirsch was shy, although she basically knew what she wanted; Bertha, on the other hand, did not put up with anything and was generally respected.

Shortly after the occupation we were required to hand over our radios, but I couldn't make up my mind to give mine up so readily. It was our only connection to the world, which we had every evening when we listened to the BBC news. The Russians threatened to punish severely anyone who did not comply with the requirement, but we did not take that so seriously. Zeumer had two radios, and since he did not want to take any risk—rightfully so—he offered me his extra radio to hand over. And so it happened. We left our radio in the living room covered with a cloth. We thought that it would be noticed less if it was out in the open, and this practice worked. All summer long we listened to the BBC in the evening as quietly as possible. Among Germans we were eventually known in the area for knowing more than other people. Often someone came who wanted to know what was going on in the world and who wanted advice about what to do—even more so when it became clear that the area would become Polish. That did not become clear until the Potsdam Treaty between the Allies.

Kreisau lies between the two Neisse rivers, the Glatz Neisse and the Görlitz Neisse. Even during the time when the penetration by the Poles, which was tolerated by the Russians, was completely obvious, it remained unclear east of which Neisse river Poland would begin and whether our area would really become Polish. In the meantime the Poles wanted to make it a foregone conclusion. First the authorities in Schweidnitz became Polish. When we had dealings with them, they were generally not unfriendly.

One day a German appeared who had been appointed the administrator of Kreisau by the Poles. By no means a malicious man, he was a man from the East, who had worked together with them. He allowed Zeumer to stay in his position and was friendly and courteous to me. He also discussed business matters with me, made sure we had bread, butter, and milk in our household, and when he was no longer allowed to deliver milk to my household, he obtained a goat for us. Zeumer, who had good qualities but had always been difficult and stubborn, and whom Helmuth had known how to handle, was tremendously angry with this man. He had to give him his house but was very comfortably accommodated in the Nieder Gräditz manor house in one of our nice new worker apartments. He had, of course, become the second man in the business, and that became difficult for him, even though he was smart enough to see that he still got off relatively well. At first it was important to this administrator to allow everything to continue to run in the existing manner, and that suited us well. But now Zeumer's and my trips over the fields came to an end and in a strangely dramatic way.

Everyone in Kreisau was familiar with the sight of Zeumer on the "spider," a light two-wheeled little cart, to which a horse was hitched. It was a dangerous looking vehicle. The seat—repaired time and again— sat like a throne, unprotected high above the wheels. With this vehicle one charged along without regard to horse, cart, and passenger over embankments, through ditches, over hill and dale, fields and meadows. Since the beginning of the war, I had accompanied Zeumer every day on one of his rounds to the various field operations, usually from one work break to the next, sometimes very early, sometimes after the lunch break. Sometimes we stayed the whole time at one place, but usually we covered a large part of the whole area. Asta, who had been driving the tractor in Kreisau since the beginning of the war in order to avoid another war work obligation, always said that the minute something went wrong, Zeumer immediately appeared on the horizon with his little cart. He was a very good administrator in his own special way. However, for my part, I was in a position to give Helmuth daily detailed reports about the status of operations and the condition of the business, and in this way he was always able to maintain very close contact to Kreisau. During these five years of the war, I did not fall a single time from this vehicle. I remember that Carl Bernd once admired that. Now one day during this summer, when we were again making our rounds, the little horse stumbled as we were going down Kirschallee. He was startled, bolted, and broke free; the shaft went up and the cart tipped over backward. Zeumer and I both went flying. I wasn't hurt but remained still for a while—actually only because I lay so comfortably and my head was throbbing. People came running anxiously, along with Zeumer, who had not been hurt. I stood up, reassured everyone and went home and lay down on my bed for a while. After that neither the opportunity nor the possibility was ever again offered to Zeumer or me to ride over the fields. During our last trip we both fell down, without suspecting it was our last.

Poles also appeared on the small farms—they took over the farms, slept in the farmers' beds, and let the Germans continue working for them. One farm after the other was taken over. Many of these Poles came from the eastern Polish areas, which had been handed over to Russia. Some German farmers were treated like slaves, others got along with "their" Poles, and almost all wanted to stay at home as long as possible in spite of this. But the village evacuations began in August. We heard about them from other areas. At our place it remained quiet for a long time.

After Marion and Muto, Romai was the next one to set out on a trip to Berlin. She was gone for a time and came back one day with identity cards for us. It was stated on these cards in five languages (German, Russian, Polish, English, and French) with a stamp and signature by the magistrate of Berlin, still at that time exclusively under Russian occupation, that our husbands had been murdered, that we were victims of Fascism, and therefore were to be treated well. She had looked around in Berlin, but for the time being there was no talk about her wanting to leave Kreisau. As usual, she had a few adventures along the way. She had gotten a ride on a Russian truck and was thrown down off the moving truck when one of the men made advances to her, and she, in turn, bit his thumb. Fortunately, there was so much shouting and noise in the back of the truck that the driver had braked and was driving slowly and so she had not really been injured. The truck simply continued on. Imagine that!

At the beginning of July something exciting happened: the western Allies moved into Berlin, occupied their respective sectors, and began to administer Berlin along with the Russians in order to establish the Control Commission for all of Germany. The Americans and the English had not been in Berlin long when Marion and Muto turned up again, having come from Kreisau. They immediately visited friends on the first evening. After dinner there was a ring at the door outside of which an English officer was standing. Why he happened to come precisely to this house, I do not know. In any case he was very concerned with finding out whether the inhabitants of the house knew anything about Helmuth Moltke's wife and his children in Silesia. When Muto and Marion said, "We came from there today!" he could hardly believe it. He had come on behalf of our friends in England, and this was his first attempt to get some information. Not until the next morning when the two women called on him in his office and again confirmed everything they had said, did he truly believe it. With that the connection to our English friends was restored.

In the meantime our Russian company in Kreisau had gotten used to us, and we to them. We knew each other, but generally the Russians didn't speak with us. But they knew exactly who we were. Once one of the soldiers said to Fräulein Hirsch that they only left us in such peace because of our husbands. Most women, and above all those who were the former fine ladies, had to work in the fields. A friendly Russian in uniform who liked our cucumbers, once came with his girlfriend, who was also in uniform, and wanted to see the "countess." I opened the door to him bare legged and in rubber boots—I had just watered the aforementioned cucumbers, and my hair was wrapped in a towel as I had just washed it. Under no circumstances would he believe that I was the "countess" and simply laughed in my face. I called Frau Pick and asked her to please tell the man who I was. He didn't believe her either. Finally I got my passport. That convinced him. He then came again once or twice. Whether because of the cucumbers or because of me was never established.

A couple of Russians had seen our pretty Liesbeth in the field and were chasing her. Liesbeth hid in the attic under big wash baskets when they rang the doorbell. They were two very nice fellows. I argued with them. I said they could not have her or visit her, but they asked if they could just *see* Liesbeth. I asked whether they would promise to leave then. Yes, they firmly promised they would do so. In that case I said I would fetch her. She came after I had convinced her to come down the stairs slowly, where, somewhat higher, she remained standing like a princess. The Russians beamed, looked at her for a while, spoke back and forth, and then nicely withdrew. We were happy that everything had gone so well and locked the doors behind them. It was probably between seven and eight in the evening.

As I was about to go up to my room, one of the Russians came down the stairs toward me, laughing, and left the house for the second time. He had just shown what he could do if he wanted to! He had climbed one of the iron poles outside that held the little corrugated iron roof, which was not attractive but was very useful for protecting the entry. Then he had climbed into the open window of the children's room and had come down through the house. Konrad, who was already in bed upstairs, still remembers the Russian who went through his room. No, he still says today, he had not been at all afraid.

All the Russians were always friendly toward the children, and they admired Konrad's beautiful curly hair, which was short but surrounded his head in soft dark blond waves. They always had to stroke it, and so for the children the Russians were not people to fear. The two Russian fellows then came several more times. They finally even sat with Liesbeth in the kitchen and played "Schwarzer Peter" with her and Frau Pick. While playing, one of them wore a top hat that he had found at our house and probably thought was half attractive, half funny. I gave it to him as a present. But someone forbade them to visit us, because after a while they no longer came. Or perhaps they had been transferred, for they didn't belong to the manor company.

After Romai was back from Berlin and the Potsdam Treaty had been made known—our radio still provided us with news every evening—it seemed to be time for me to go to Berlin as well, to write letters, speak with friends, and get advice about the future. Although it had gone well for us up until then, it still seemed certain that in time we would have to leave. We were completely shut off from the West. Of course, I had always sent messages for my mother with people who were trying to get through to western Germany from Silesia. But we heard nothing. There was no mail, and the trains ran very irregularly.

Before I left I had another typical experience. During the course of the summer the Poles had set up a kind of militia. They usually recruited people who had worked as forced laborers in Germany. They were people who had suffered greatly in Germany, and one could see the hate written on their faces. These Poles were a completely different type from the ones who took over the land around us. Most of them were probably also active Communists. They were the ones who beat people, locked them up, and harassed them. The Germans complained about the militia a lot, and sometimes the Poles did too. One such militiaman came to us during this time and demanded our identity cards in a coarse and impudent tone. I don't know what angered me so much about him. It was probably simply his impertinent manner. I said I did not allow anyone to talk to me in such a way in my house, and asked what gave him the right to demand our identity cards. If he could not behave politely, I would show him nothing at all but rather would make a complaint about him. He was furious and threatened me with his revolver. But I knew for sure he would not shoot and said, "Get out of my house!" I can still hear Frau Pick's quietly murmured and appalled "Countess Moltke!" She watched the scene while standing in the kitchen door. The man put his revolver away, gave me a resounding slap, and left.

With one red and one pale cheek I ran immediately to the Russian captain in the manor. I was afraid to leave the children behind at the mercy of capricious Polish acts. I said to the somewhat surprised captain that I had to go to Berlin for matters having to do with my husband. This—showing him my cheek—just happened to me. I asked whether I could put the children and our house under his protection while I was gone in case the Poles came again. The captain said yes without hesitating, and I was truly relieved and reassured. The Russians didn't like the Poles, sided with the Germans when in doubt, and treated the Poles badly. Indeed the Russian protection soon proved to be effective.

The best way to travel to Berlin was to leave from Waldenburg. After the end of the war the first trains loaded with coal began traveling from the Waldenburg coal-mining area. Once a coal train was assembled, it departed. Now and again a couple of empty freight cars were attached because there were soldiers to be transported or perhaps because so many women and children wanted to travel along. The railway men in these trains were still Germans. When Frau Raschke, our neighbor and farmer's wife (the Berghaus belonged to the part of the village called Nieder-Gräditz, and therefore we had farmers as our direct neighbors on both sides), heard that I wanted to go to Berlin, she asked if she could come along. Her mother lived in Berlin, and she wanted to check on her. That was fine with me.

I left the children well protected in the Berghaus and started out with Frau Raschke. In Waldenburg we even succeeded in finding room in a closed car, and already in the late afternoon of the very same day, our train departed. However, halfway there, probably past Görlitz in Niederlausitz, we were thrown out—the car was being deployed as a Russian transport. There we stood in the middle of the night, and there was nothing else for us to do but climb somewhere onto the coal. That was not so bad for us, but there were families in the car with small children, baby carriages, and luggage; they all had to climb onto the coal. It was a warm August night, there was a bright starry sky and the air was magnificent; we weren't freezing. We both found room way up front, rather high up on a pile of coal. We did become sleepy around morning—that was dangerous since one could easily fall down from the coal while sleeping. However, there was enough excitement to keep us from falling asleep.

A Russian guard was responsible for the train. As soon as the train stopped anywhere, thieves jumped on immediately. The coal and the luggage of travelers was of great value at the time. The thieves waited in the stations for these trains and then made a haul. We often heard them rummaging around near us. Then the people on the coal screamed and called out, and the watchmen answered by shooting into the air several times. That didn't seem to make much of an impression on the thieves, for soon there would be scratching somewhere, and the whole thing started all over again, keeping us awake. We continued a ways into daybreak, and around seven o'clock we were in Nieder-Schöneweide, a suburb of Berlin. From there we could take the city train—it was running.

In Berlin I stayed in Marion and Peter's little house that we had grown fond of on Hortensienstrasse. Even though the house had been damaged by bombs, it was still livable. The ss occupants had left everything behind, the Russian wave had passed over it, and then an older plumber and his wife, who had worked for the Yorcks, had immediately moved in. So it happened that everything appeared unchanged. Many practical utensils had probably been stolen, but everything else was still there, and so right away we again had a proper home in Berlin. Marion and Muto were traveling, and I slept in the living room. I wrote again to my mother and for the first time also to my brother Carl in Switzerland, to Lionel Curtis in England, and to Dorothy Thompson in the United States. I looked for German friends whom I thought were in Berlin, made contact with the English and the Americans, and asked them to expedite my letters. In this way I came into contact with the oss-Office of Strategic Services, which was in Dahlem. There I met Allen Dulles, some friendly officers, and Gero von Schulze-Gaevernitz. They all knew about us. They had me tell them about the conditions in Silesia and were quite skeptical when I said that I wanted to go back once more.

I also had a request addressed to a Communist who was one of the leaders of the Berlin party. In one of our neighboring villages, Faulbrück, an old Communist, had survived the Nazi period. One day this man called on me, and we had maintained a loose connection during the following months. Now he wanted to know from the Communists in Berlin how one should act toward the Poles and Russians in Silesia, whether one should stay or leave. I went into the party building of the KPD (Kommunistishe Partei Deutschlands) near the Spittelmarkt. After a short wait the man received me and rather hesitatingly gave information. Hesitating most likely because the party itself was not yet sure how it would act, and the evacuations of Silesia were just beginning to get serious. All he really said was that the Communists should act as everyone else did.

To be on the safe side, I registered the children and myself with the police in Berlin as residing at 50 Hortensienstrasse. Then I was ready for the trip back. However, a Swede had told me that the Reichwein children could possibly go to Sweden soon if they wanted to. I should wait to find out for sure. So I stayed a day or two longer. I was longing to see the Poelchau apartment on Afrikanische Strasse in Tegel but did not expect to find the Poelchaus in Berlin. They had planned to wait for the end at their friends', the Truchesses, in northern Bavaria. Herr Truchess had also been imprisoned in Tegel, and Harald had become friends with him. I just wanted to see this apartment that had become so dear to me in the months before Helmuth's death and where I had almost "lived" with Helmuth. It was still somewhat difficult to get there, but the subway finally went to the Seestrasse station and then there was a tram along Müllerstrasse. I climbed the many stairs in the building—

the Poelchaus lived on the top floor. I rang and waited. Gertie Siemsen, a friend of the Poelchaus, opened the door. She lived there with her baby, born at the beginning of May. She said immediately, "Do you know who's living here? Your brother-in-law Wend!"

Today one can hardly imagine how astonishing it was that we found each other in this way. I had of course heard nothing from him, nor had I seen him since he left Schweidnitz at the beginning of February—it was now the end of August. Shortly thereafter he had been run over and injured by a German army vehicle; he could not walk and was brought to a hospital in the Lausitz region. There the advancing Russians had recently released him from the hospital—sick men were of no interest to them. He had traveled to Berlin and tried from there to get to Asta in the West. Asta knew nothing about his whereabouts. We were both very happy and relieved to see each other. Wend had nothing, and I also had nothing that could be useful to him, but a pair of socks from Marion or Muto came just at the right time for him! We spent the last day together, and on the next morning he accompanied me and Frau Raschke to Nieder-Schöneweide, from where the empty coal cars were supposed to travel back to Waldenburg.

The Americans had provided me with U.S. soldier rations. They were concerned that I really wanted to go back to Silesia. The Germans assured me I would not be successful, for now the Oder and the Görlitz Neisse formed the new border between countries—the Poles were throwing the Germans out and definitely weren't letting any more in. This information was not very encouraging, but my children were a powerful draw, and Frau Raschke felt she was in the same situation.

Thus began the most adventuresome trip I had ever experienced. It was also characteristic for the conditions of that time, and for people in general, for it was full of both pleasant and unpleasant experiences. For that reason it is well worth telling.

The trip lasted three days and three nights. At first everything went smoothly—there were empty coal cars, and the weather was nice and warm. Now and again we waited here and there for a while but not all that long. We probably crossed the border around noon. At first it turned out to be a simple crossing, but several kilometers later the train stopped at a station. Polish militia came into the cars and threw out all

Germans with the exception of German soldiers, who had been released from the West to return to Silesia. Strangely enough they still let them travel home then.

A large group of complaining people was assembling at the station and was being driven away like a herd by Poles with long cracking whips. We were among them. I tried to figure out how I could make myself noticed. I called repeatedly to one of the men with whips and said over and over again, "I have international papers!" That wasn't quite true, but it had an effect. He took notice and sent me to a young militia lieutenant, who had something resembling an office in the area. So for the time being we were out of the crowd.

I immediately saw that the lieutenant also had the hate-filled expression that was typical of so many of these militia people. I showed him the nice papers procured by Romai and another written confirmation I had obtained from the Berlin magistrate, which said I had been in Berlin in matters concerning my husband and must now return to Silesia to my children. The militiaman inspected all of that, mocked and made fun of the downfallen countess, thought it over, and then said: fine, I could continue, but this woman—pointing to Frau Raschke—she had to go back. Good Frau Raschke immediately cried out loudly and full of despair, "Don't abandon me, don't abandon me! I must come too!" What a commotion! So I said we both had to go to Silesia. If we wanted to stay together, he said, then we would both have to go back. At this point I opened my backpack somewhat despairingly and attempted to bargain. They did not want provisions—those they had—but six (!) American cigarettes, which were part of the rations, would be enough. I also offered him a yellow rain cape made of plastic and clearly recall that an older Pole in the group took the cape, carefully folded it, and stuck it in my backpack again behind the officer's back.

We could hardly believe that we could really go. We went back to the train as fast as we could, climbed into a car, and sat there exhausted and as quiet as little mice. We were hardly inside when another Polish raid took place, and they threw us out again—nothing we said helped. But the militia lieutenant was standing on the platform, recognized us, and let us get in again. After a while there was a violent jolt, and the train actually began to move toward the east. It was a heavenly feeling.

We now believed we had everything behind us, but it was still not so easy.

Besides us and others, there were two released soldiers sitting in the closed freight car. One was a bank official from the Waldenburg area, the other was a farmer from Upper Silesia. The latter could speak Polish. Although we had departed and gone forward a bit, we were soon stopped again. During the night, when we stopped, dark characters came time after time into our car, looked for things, and aimed their lights on us. Then the farmer would say over and over again, "We are Poles!" With that we were left alone. The two soldiers had joined us, and we were now all four traveling together. Frau Raschke and I were so exhausted that we were sleeping quite peacefully on the floor of the car, our heads on our backpacks.

The next morning we discovered that we were only in Sorau. That is north of Sagan, about two and a half train hours away from Berlin on the Berlin-Frankfurt Oder-Liegnitz line, on which we usually traveled to Silesia. We had already been waiting there for many hours. Sitting on this one-track line, which had formerly consisted of four tracks in some parts (the Russians had dismantled all the tracks in the first months), one had the impression that the freight trains were piling up one after the other so that we would be stalled for days. We thought we would probably progress more quickly by taking the road and decided to get out. As we were vigorously marching off along the road from Sorau to Sagan, a whole line of empty horse carts with small Russian or Polish farm horses passed us. We were now quite used to these carts, so typical of the East. At first the German soldiers used them, then the Russians, and now the Poles. In contrast to our heavy field wagons these carts were very light and pulled by slender little horses. On our roads and unloaded, they literally danced along the street in the quick rhythm of their trotting horses.

We let the whole line go by us until we finally had the courage to wave at one of the last carts. The Polish driver stopped immediately; without saying or asking much he let the four of us get on, and we went quickly and cheerfully nonstop to the station in Sagan, where the wagon convoy was to be loaded. We were lucky in every respect, for had we been going on foot we probably would have been stopped by

Poles and put into a work gang, which they had set up everywhere for cleanup work. Whoever was apprehended, often had to work there for weeks before he could continue on. We did pass such a roadblock.

In this way we arrived in one piece at the Sagan railway station. It was just as hopelessly crowded with trains as the Sorau station—there were freight trains with dismantled machines, old tanks, and such, which were to be transported to Russia but were full to the brim with people. There were a few Germans and many Russians and Poles who came from Germany and wanted to go back to their homes. They looked at us crossly when we tried to climb into the already full freight car with them and forbade us to do so. And yet I remember a small Polish or Russian girl, who unexpectedly, all on her own, slipped me a piece of bread.

As we were helplessly going back and forth on the crowded platform, two armed Russian soldiers came straight up to Frau Raschke and me and waved at us to come with them. That was not at all nice, and our courage fell. The two German soldiers came with us, unasked and unimpeded. We went through the point of entry. What else could we do but follow? Why had they picked us out of all the people from the anonymous crowd? What could that mean? That worried us as we went down the stairs through the depot and out of the station. They led us a few steps along the railway station building and then again into another door on the corner of the building. There was an office, and Frau Raschke and I were shown with gestures that we were to clean it. Frau Raschke did so excellently, I less so but still not so poorly that the Russians would have noticed. In the meantime the two soldiers kept busy polishing a motorcycle, and after about an hour we were finished. The Russians were very pleased and regretted that they were not able to pay us for our labor. They told us, however, which of the many trains would be the first to leave, and that was truly helpful.

This train was also full of people and machines. A Russian lieutenant stood on a flat car, onto which a tank had been loaded; next to him was a young Russian woman. We made modest signs to the Russian man, for in front of the tank was a nice empty little spot, where all four of us could have sat. The Russian refused, but apparently we had an advocate in the woman. She talked to him, and finally he nodded with his head and we climbed on gratefully. By now we had also gotten used to the completely different feeling toward time in the East, which had moved into Silesia with the Russians and the Poles. Waiting was a part of life. We patiently resigned ourselves to the inevitable. I no longer know how long it was until the train departed; I only remember that in the last moment a Russian soldier jumped onto the car and went a ways with us. He immediately lay down, wrapped himself in his coat, and went to sleep. Later he woke up, took bread and a crumpled bag of sugar out of his coat pocket, ate both together, and gave us some of it without saying a word.

We would travel a short distance and then stop again, often between stations. Then everyone would jump out of the cars, run into the fields, and look for potatoes. With stones they built small campfire rings alongside the train, boiled water in tin cans, and roasted the potatoes in the ashes. We did the same and shared our provisions. When the train was able to continue, it whistled twice, allowing the people time to clean up and get back on between the two whistles, and then moved on. We did not get to Liegnitz on this evening. We had to spend the night again waiting on a side track. I slept behind the tank. I had more room there, but the night was cooler and around morning I felt queasy. I froze miserably. Then near the engine I saw a big, beautiful fire. I was miserable and wanted to warm up. So I went over hill and dale along the train to the fire. The engineer, a Pole, and one enormous Russian soldier were sitting there. When they saw me approaching so slowly, they brought a wooden log near the fire so that I could also sit there, and gave me warm potatoes and tea, which the Pole brewed with water from the engine. They were very friendly without being able, or even wanting, to speak a word to me. All of that combined did me so much good that I was able to return to my tank car after a short time feeling well and comfortable.

Finally it became light. We were still stopped at the same spot when suddenly a passenger train appeared out of nowhere—so it seemed—whistling and making a lot of noise. Although it was completely full, it stopped, and with quick determination we changed trains. We had to climb onto the roof of a passenger car, for people were already hanging in bunches at the doorways. But it was still empty on the roofs, and we thought nothing of climbing up there. Again the sun was shining, and we traveled through the country, rattling and whistling, with a lot of smoke. We felt like kings up there, just carefully pulling in our heads under the bridges, and after about an hour we were in Liegnitz.

I had not seen the Liegnitz railway station since the end of January. It was in terrible condition—an enormous sewer. We were hoping for more good luck in Liegnitz. But not a soul there knew when and to which destination a train would depart. Although some engines were switching tracks in the station, even their engineers didn't know where they would eventually be sent, and the few that did depart were not going in our direction. It was only fifty-six kilometers from Liegnitz to Kreisau. If necessary, we could manage that on foot, but again we had lost a lot of time waiting; we were tired and preferred to sleep one more night. We found accommodations, after a fashion, in a house that belonged to a priest's office, but all four of us had to sleep on the floor, and that was already the third night.

So the next morning we set out very early and went on foot to Jauer. That took several hours. We had no obstacles to overcome, but I was exhausted and hungry. For although I still had a small reserve of American rations, they had not been intended for three days and three nights, and I didn't want to use everything in case I was held up even longer. I stayed a little behind the others and finally went into a house and asked if I could get something to drink. The farmer's wife still had the remains of breakfast sitting there and said I should feel free to finish up the fried potatoes. With that she gave me some herbal tea to drink that was still warm in a pot on the stove. Those two things revived me like food fit for the gods. However, when we arrived at the Jauer railway station, we preferred, in the eastern manner, to wait for a train rather than walk farther. Like the other people we sat on the platform, let our legs dangle over the rails, and waited.

It was not at all long until a truly beautiful passenger train arrived. We could even get right on and find a spot. The train actually traveled quietly and without many stops—considering that we were now on a branch line—passing through Striegau, Königszelt, and Schweidnitz, and before reaching Kamenz, stopped like a well-behaved train in Kreisau. So we arrived between six and seven o'clock in the evening.

Everything was perfectly peaceful. When we went up the Berghaus hill, Caspar came running to me. "Oh, there you are again Reialie!" he called happily, as though I had only been away a couple of hours. The Berghaus appeared to me like a peaceful island in a rough sea.

However, they had also not been completely without difficulties there. The Poles, four of them, had come again and this time Romai had opened the door to them. However, she had already sent her Roland, who was then almost nine years old, to the Russian captain in the manor. Roland had jumped out the window and run the five minutes to the manor; ten minutes later four armed Russians appeared, and the Poles immediately retreated. In the meantime the first administrator on the farm had disappeared, and a proper Pole had moved in. Zeumer had an even more difficult time with him, but toward us he behaved in a not unfriendly manner. In the future the farm was to be administered as a property of the Polish state.

After my return from Berlin we experienced another fine affair with our captain in the manor. At the beginning of the summer our Wierischau renter, who had come to take refuge from the bombs and whose large family had already departed at the beginning of February, had brought us his charming young curly haired black spaniel before leaving to join his family. The Russians probably thought this pretty animal, with its black silky curls, was just as beautiful as Konrad with his curly hair, and we soon noticed that they were after the dog. But the children also loved him, and so we watched him very carefully. But finally, one day at the end of the summer, he was gone. Where could he be? Soon Roland Reichwein figured it out—there was barking in the manor! What should we do now? We did not want to upset the captain, but we also didn't want to have the dog simply taken from us. Romai and I went to the manor together and asked to speak to the captain. We waited a little while. Then a female Russian civil servant, who was supposed to interpret, took us up to him.

The captain sat upstairs in the hall, as one would imagine a Persian satrap, in the giant gold armchair covered with black damask. It was said about this chair that the even more gigantic and very fat Uncle Ludwig Moltke from Wernersdorf could not get up from it without help. So the satrap was sitting there looking grim, for he knew exactly that we came because of the dog. But now came our trick, and it did wonders. I asked the interpreter to tell the Herr Captain that it would give us pleasure to give him the dog as a gift! The captain jumped up immediately, smiling and happy. We had to tell him the name of the dog. "Rago," he carefully repeated. He asked whether the dog had a bloodline, and whether he was trained to hunt. I explained to him that at best a bloodline could still be found in Wierischau, and he arranged to go there with me.

Now that he was so obviously in high spirits, Romai asked if she could perhaps take two beds, which belonged to her and which she needed, to the Berghaus, since it was said the company was soon to move to Schweidnitz. The captain replied in the friendliest manner that they were pulling out in the next few days and everything would stay and remain exactly the way it was. Then Romai could take what she wanted. In this way Rago sealed the friendly relations we had had during this summer with "our" captain. Already on the next day, the Russians did indeed pull out. But when we went to the manor afterward it was completely cleared out. There was nothing left except two small beautiful wardrobes from the eighteenth century that belonged to Asta and Wend—the only truly good pieces that had still been in the manor. The wind was whistling through the empty manor!

In Berlin Gero Gaevernitz told me that a number of people must still be living in his parents' country house in the Neurode district. He had not heard anything from them in the last few years, as he and his family had gone to the United States, and he was concerned about them. He wanted to know how everything looked there, wanted to send his friends his regards—and to have someone tell them that they should leave Silesia. He had asked if I could possibly look in on them. The Neurode district is situated in the middle of the mountains, not in front of them as is the Schweidnitz district. There was no train connection, and we could no longer risk going by bicycle. The Russians no longer took the bicycles, but the Poles did, and in the meantime all Germans in Silesia had to wear white armbands. We didn't wear them but in not doing so risked getting into trouble.

Some time after my return from Berlin—Marion and Muto were once again with us—Marion and I wanted to visit the Gaevernitz house.

I have the most pleasant memories of this journey too. It was far—farther than we had expected. We had set out when the sun came up, and although we had not stopped anywhere for long, we did not arrive until the late afternoon. We found a magnificent manor house in a large park; Helmuth had been a guest there numerous times. Poles occupied the big house; the people Gaevernitz was concerned about lived in the neighboring houses. They were reasonably well off. They had had experiences with Russians and Poles similar to ours. They were happy to see us and happy about our connection to Gaevernitz. We spent the night there and went back the next day via a different route. In all it was forty-five kilometers, and our feet resented having to walk so much within two days. In spite of sturdy shoes they were full of blisters, but otherwise the excursion did us good.

Our feet had just healed when Romai came rushing into the house one day to tell us that there were Americans in the village, and they wanted to visit us. She was quite excited, and just as we were coming out of the house, a big American sports car drove up and Gaevernitz got out. An American soldier, who spoke fluent Polish and Russian, came with him as his chauffeur. Gaevernitz had been able to get permission from the Russians and Poles to go to Silesia, and he had decided to see about his house in Neurode himself. They spent the night with us, went to the house the next day, and returned in the evening.

The Americans wanted to find out as much as possible about the conditions in Silesia. They had already asked us for a detailed report in Berlin, which we had been working on in the meantime. The systematic evacuations from Silesia had seriously gotten underway only in the last few weeks. Now Gaevernitz wanted to form his own impression. He asked if we could accompany him the next day to Breslau where we had connections to Catholic and Protestant clergy. At that time in Silesia the churches formed the only network through which somewhat reliable news could be passed on, and it was only through them that connections to individual places could be maintained.

Marion and I were happy to travel by car through the country, to be able to look at it closely, and to see Breslau. But our impressions were not comforting. Behind the front where the Russians had stopped until the end of the war, everything was destroyed, riddled with bullets, and devastated. To be sure, we saw that even here evacuees had returned and were trying to start over in the rubble, but the destruction was immense, the land was not tilled, and weeds grew in the beautiful fields. I now saw, for the first time, the great difference between these two zones. The city of Breslau was just as shocking: driving in from the south we saw only ruins. However, the center of the city was rather well preserved. We met the people to whom we had been directed, had a look at the destroyed city in which it appeared that only a few shacks had life in them—although in reality thousands of people were still living there— and drove back in the afternoon via Strehlen-Reichenbach.

It had already gotten dark when we reached Kreisau. Before we arrived at the Berghaus hill, we were stopped by some inhabitants of the village. They said we should be careful—there were Poles at the Berghaus. They had driven up there with an empty box cart some time ago. Russians were also up there. This was not exactly pleasant for the Americans. But they understood that we wanted to go there as fast as possible and unhesitatingly decided not to leave us in the lurch. Dressed in a beautiful American colonel's uniform, Gaevernitz was anything but a soldier; but on this evening he conducted himself as a soldier. I can still see how he took a deep breath in front of our door. But then he was excellent. The Poles and Russians were simply flabbergasted to see an American officer in front of them. The house was indeed full of Poles, who were examining everything. The children were sitting together with Frau Pick in the kitchen and were being guarded, that is, protected, by a Russian soldier with a big walrus moustache who was sitting comfortably on the kitchen chair with a rifle in his hand. Muto and Romai were busy in the house.

This is what happened: the Poles had come and said that we had walled in valuables in the basement of the house. Now they wanted to take them away. In fact, with the help of a Polish bricklayer (this was the man, by the way, who had said that if I was staying, he would stay too), I had walled in linens, clothes, silver, and books under the basement stairs of our Berghaus and under the basement stairs of the manor. I had done this not only for us, but also for those who had already left because of the onslaught of German soldiers who were streaming back and who were in such a destructive mood.

The things under the manor stairs are probably still there today and long since decayed. In the summer the Russians had merrily cooked in front of this wall and had noticed nothing, although Russians usually had a feeling for such tricks. They also would not have profited all that much from clearing it out, for the Moltkes did not possess any treasures, and what was valuable to them would not have interested the Russians and Poles. In the Berghaus the Poles had torn down the wall and taken everything upstairs where it lay in wild disarray. Apparently they were somewhat disappointed about what they had found and were still rummaging around in my papers upstairs.

The Americans had come at the right time. They stopped the Poles, and Gaevernitz, with the help of his interpreter, made it clear to them that they had no right to take our things, and they were to kindly leave everything behind and withdraw. That made an impression, but there was still some negotiating back and forth and finally Gaevernitz's interpreter went with them back to Schweidnitz, where they had come from, in order to discuss the matter with their superiors once again. He returned after about an hour. Yes, all was well, I could keep everything. My typewriter had been the most difficult object—they had fought over that the longest.

Incidentally, they had not noticed the radio. It survived the raid in its usual spot. However, the presence of uniformed American soldiers in Schweidnitz had caused a stir, and early the next morning two Russians came and demanded the identification papers of the Americans. I was in the room and naturally couldn't understand anything but could tell that my two friends did not feel at ease. The Russians checked everything for some time. There were all kinds of things to discuss, but finally they left. They were barely out of the house when Gaevernitz confessed to me that his authorization to travel to Poland had already expired. He had worked that out with the border officials, but to make matters worse, the permit had not been given to him but rather to another officer. This man had not been able to make the trip, so Gaevernitz had used the opportunity and had traveled under a false name. If that came out things could turn out badly for everyone. They had to leave—as quickly as possible—so that the Schweidnitz Russians had no opportunity to inspect the papers a second time.

The two men, pale and nervous, got into their beautiful car. I gave Gaevernitz the first bundle of Helmuth's letters, which had been hidden so long from the Nazis back in my beehives. Gaevernitz leaned out of the car once more and said, "You must all get out of here, as quickly as possible. You are sitting on top of a volcano here!" With that he left. He and his companion arrived at the border without any obstacles, crossed it smoothly, and reached Berlin.

From all we had experienced it became clear that we could not remain in Silesia for the long term. However, we thought it made sense to hold our position for a while longer, especially since we felt solidarity with all the other villagers. We were certain that the children's paradise of the summer could not last through the winter. During spring, after the manor inhabitants had left, I had the remaining coal transported to the Berghaus, but more was unobtainable. Therefore, it was smarter to take the children out of Kreisau in good time.

First Romai made preparations with her four children. She organized, packed, bundled up and divided her loads, and loaded herself with an unbelievable burden. After the loss of her possessions in Berlin, she had, with great energy, under difficult and unpleasant conditions, rebuilt a new and nice household in the manor. With that same energy and tenacity she now assumed the responsibility for the transport of her children and as many belongings as possible. The plan was for her to see that her children were well cared for and then to return to Kreisau once more so that I could take my children away. We accompanied the family to the Kreisau train station and waited patiently until a train came. With bag and baggage they found room and disappeared.

So now our household had dwindled down. After the visit from Gaevernitz, perhaps one or two weeks had gone by when we again experienced something very unusual. We had just sold goods in Schweidnitz for Polish money. The German money that we had was no longer of any use. We could not manage for much longer without Polish money, but of course we had all kinds of things to sell. Probably the first things to go were a piece of silk and a pair of women's shoes Carl Bernd had sent from Greece to Kreisau for my safekeeping. Marion accompanied me again. It is only a good hour to Schweidnitz if one goes cross county over the Mühlberg. One heads straight for the high spire of the Schweidnitz main church, which beckons in a friendly manner. In this way the trip does not seem so long.

At that time the astonishing thing was how quickly and how dramatically Schweidnitz had changed during the six months since the war. Now it looked completely Polish. This was partly so because of the new Polish signs and street names and postwar troubles of all kinds. It was also because of the different people on the street and the completely changed lifestyle they brought with them. I would never have thought it possible that such a change could have occurred so quickly. We completed our business very successfully, we thought. Polish money jingled in our pockets as we went home. On the way to the Berghaus, through the farm, people called to us. They said we had company again. This time they were from England. I couldn't believe it, but one woman was absolutely sure. Yes, they had personally asked her the way, and they were now up there. We took long strides, and indeed—on our narrow driveway there was a small unmistakable English four-seater, complete with a little British flag. What a sight deep in Silesia among Russians and Poles.

Inside the house we found two just as unmistakable English gentlemen, who were warmly conversing with Muto: Mr. Hancock and Mr. Finch from the British embassy in Warsaw. How these men, after all the war years, impressed me with their English shirts, their English jackets, and their English mannerisms! Another world—and yet one that was so familiar to me—seemed to have fallen out of the clouds into our Berghaus. Their appearance was the answer to my letter written in Berlin to Lionel Curtis. He now tried to move heaven and earth to help us out of Kreisau. He had turned to Ernest Bevin, the British foreign minister. Bevin had made inquires about us and had come to Con O'Neill in the foreign office, of all people, who knew Helmuth from Berlin and regarded him highly. After receiving the information, Bevin had asked [British Field Marshall and Allied Commander] Montgomery in Berlin to ask the Russians and Poles whether the English might pick us up from Kreisau.

The two Englishmen had come to Kreisau to tell me this. They had other business in the Liegnitz area and then wanted to return to Warsaw as quickly as possible. Consequently, they only stayed for lunch and spoke seriously with us. They didn't know if picking us up would be allowed, and they had no way of communicating to me the result of the British intervention. I should wait for four weeks. If no one came by then, it meant that the English petition was denied; then I must promise to leave Kreisau on my own. Before they left, the senior officer, Mr. Hancock, drew me into a corner. Like a father he asked me if I had enough Polish money. I explained how I was able to obtain it. But that did not seem good enough for him. He gave me the equivalent of fifty pounds in zloty, and I gave him a receipt made out to the British embassy, Warsaw. Later I was able to pay that back from England, but at that time it seemed like a fairy tale to me. Then our two friends departed.

Now we also finally lost the radio, and that to the funny Russian with the walrus moustache who had watched the children in the kitchen during the Polish visit. At that time Mr. Serpuchov had taken a good look into our pantry and discovered that we had a great deal of homemade jam. He then came every few days and fetched himself another jar of jam, as tribute. Apparently it tasted delicious to him, and he consumed a considerable amount. One day he came with a mysterious face. He had heard from the Poles that in the evening at our house there was a "turulurulu" sound. So we had a radio! "Upstairs," he said, and went on a search. At first we acted like we didn't understand him, and in the meantime we were thinking of how to get out of this situation. The Russian made a drastic sign: if we didn't hand over the radio—rrr—slash our throats! Better to hand it over!

We knew in the meantime that we could not remain anyway. Was it better to admit that we had a radio or to secretly throw the thing in the bushes? This was not so simple, and we discussed the matter while the Russian was searching the house. We decided that we would rather give it to him because we already knew him and did not have to be afraid of him. We brought him into the kitchen. He came and saw it and was enthusiastic, beaming like an overjoyed child. When he turned it on and actually heard music, he was beside himself with joy and actually danced around in the kitchen. After a while he composed himself somewhat and gave us instructions to put it away again and hide it until the evening. When night fell, another unknown Russian came on a motorcycle. He had several blankets in which he carefully wrapped our radio. He then strapped it onto the motorcycle and disappeared with it. We had gotten rid of it in the best way—unofficially as private Russian booty.

Now the last weeks in Kreisau were upon us. Marion and Muto went to Berlin again. In their place Davy came to Silesia, by way of Kreisau. However, she did not go back to Wernersdorf, where everything was destroyed, but rather to Bresa, where she remained for many months until the evacuation of the whole area. Then the children and I were alone again with Frau Pick and Liesbeth. The fall weeks were very peaceful and beautiful—a sunny, calm October. I had the feeling that time was once again standing still. Nothing disturbed us; we heard nothing and were not worried. My right index finger was painfully infected and had to be opened up in the hospital in Schweidnitz. The wound, which was healing poorly, disabled me, and it was not at all possible—until it healed—to undertake the trip with the children to Berlin across the difficult border, where everything was taken from the people. We could only wait, and it was wonderful to wait. I do not recall why I was still on the farm, for I no longer had anything to do there. In any case, I had been in the pigpen in Nieder-Gräditz and was coming out of the door when Caspar came running to the farm and called out in his high-pitched voice, "Come on, Reialie, we have to go! The Englishmen are here!"

Four weeks to the day had passed since the car from Warsaw had been here. The English men had come with a large passenger car and a small truck. The truck was half full of emergency equipment. The friendly Major Caird and his two soldiers felt like they were on a military expedition in enemy territory. I had trouble convincing them that it was all right to spend the night in our beds instead of setting up their tents. But they finally gave in while I packed. There were still a lot of things in suitcases in the house from the Polish visit. It spread like wildfire in the village that we were now leaving. Although they had told me that at the most I could take only my things, I also took a whole lot of other suitcases along. Everything that we still have from Kreisau today, we owe to the English.

It still bothers me that I refused to take along an enormous accordion belonging to the young letter carrier, Herr Jung, which he brought over on a handcart. However, there were too many things to stow that seemed important at the time. Only the children and I were supposed to go along, but the friendly major had pity at the end for good Frau Pick. She was allowed to come with us.

We set out early the next morning. The house was left unlocked. We drove down the hill toward Eule Mountain. When the car started up I asked Caspar, "When do you think we'll return?" "In one year!" he said, cheerfully and firmly. We traveled along the bumpy, narrow road to the train station, drove over the Peile bridge, past the chapel hill, past the mill, the school, and Sister Ida's *Spielschule*, along the wall of the cow shed, past the farmyard gate, where we saw the farm and the manor, then farther through the village to Gräditz, where we took the high road to Schweidnitz. Seven hours later we were in Berlin. At the border the Poles greeted us, opened the barrier, and, thanks to the friendship of the English, we crossed unhindered over the Polish-German border, that was feared by all at the time.

Afterword

The first two sections were read critically by my two sons, my grand-daughter Dorothea, Sabine Reichwein, and Peter Hoffmann, all of whom also offered many helpful suggestions. It was a gift for me to once again express myself in the wonderful German language—how do the Germans come by such a magnificent language? I would not have done it without the repeated requests from Ernst-Peter Wieckenberg.

The third section, the description of the last months in Kreisau, originated in 1961 and appeared in 1984.[1] And now a completely new Kreisau/Krzyżowa is to evolve. Friends of the resistance against dictatorships in Germany and in Poland have gotten together and have founded the "Kreisau Foundation for European Understanding," which owns the farm complex and the Berghaus. The governments have provided the means for the building renovation. Kreisau is to be designated again as a place for meetings, for speaking and listening, and above all, as a place where younger and older people can meet. Kreisau will now, should now, and can now promote a better coexistence in Europe.

---

[1] Freya von Moltke, Michael Balfour, Julian Frisby: Helmuth James Graf von Moltke 1907–1945. Berlin, 1984 (cf. p.8)—C. H. Beck.

Glossary

Adenauer, Konrad (1876–1967). One of Germany's most important political leaders in the post–World War II period. He served as chancellor from 1949 to 1963.

Balfour, Michael (1908–1995). Historian and author of numerous histories and biographies. He was a close friend of Helmuth von Moltke and the author of *Helmuth von Moltke: A Leader against Hitler.*

Bevin, Ernest (1881–1951). Powerful British union leader, minister of labor and national service in Churchill's government, and foreign secretary after World War II.

Brüning, Heinrich (1885–1970). Conservative German statesman and chancellor from 1930 to 1932, before Hitler's appointment.

Curtis, Lionel (1872–1955). Influential public administrator, author, and advocate of a federal world order. He is credited with replacing the term *empire* with *commonwealth.*

Dulles, Allen (1893–1969). United States diplomat and expert in the field of intelligence. He headed the Office of Strategic Services, an intelligence service, in Bern from 1942 to 1945.

Field marshal. The highest-ranking officer in the German army, just below the commander in chief.

Frisby, Julian. He came to Kreisau from England to learn German and became a close family friend of the von Moltkes.

Gleichschaltung. The Nazi policy of eliminating institutions of the Weimar Republic that were not useful to the National Socialists and strengthening those that were. This process was carried out with a great deal of violence and bloodshed.

Gördeler, Carl Friedrich (1884–1945). Lawyer and civil servant, mayor of

Leipzig, and later Reich commissioner for price control. He was actively involved in plans to overthrow Hitler and was to play a leading role in the new government after the coup. He was arrested in August 1944 and executed in February 1945.

Gründerzeit. The years of rapid industrial expansion (1871–1873) in Germany after Bismarck's consolidation of the Empire.

Halder, Franz (1884–1972). Career officer, Chief of General Staff of the Army (1938–1942). His plans for a coup in 1938 were never carried out. He was arrested in 1944 and imprisoned in a concentration camp from 1944 to 1945.

Harnack, Arvid (1901–1942). Lawyer and civil servant in the Ministry of Economics and one of the leaders of the "Red Band" or "Red Orchestra" resistance group, which was active in 1941 and 1942. Harnack was executed in December 1942.

Hindenburg, Paul von (1847–1934). A field marshal during World War I and president of the Weimar Republic from 1925 to 1934. Although Hindenburg distrusted Hitler, he appointed him chancellor in 1933, thinking he could be easily controlled.

Kommunistische Partei Deutschlands (KPD). The Communist Party of Germany.

Landrat. The head of the administration of a "Kreis," or district.

Maass, Hermann (1897–1944). Social Democrat and trade-union leader. He frequently passed copies of Hitler's speeches to the Western press. He was arrested in August 1944 and executed in October 1944.

Montgomery, Bernard Law (1887–1976). British field marshal and Allied Commander in World War II.

Oberkommando der Wehrmacht (OKW). The High Command of the Armed Forces.

Opelfrosch. A make of car. "Frosch" means frog.

Röhm-Putsch, Ernst (1887–1934). The leader of Hitler's storm troopers (SA). He was murdered by the members of Hitler's personal guard (SS) on 30 June 1934 along with other members of the SA and various political enemies of Hitler's. Hitler feared that the SA was becoming too powerful.

Schmid, Carlo (1896–1979). Senior administrative officer stationed in France. He acted as an intermediary between Helmuth von Moltke and the French Resistance.

Schulze-Boysen, Harro (1909–1942). Lieutenant in the Ministry of Aviation.

He led the Red Band resistance group with Harnack. Executed in December 1942.

Schulze-Gaevernitz, Gero von. Assistant to Allen Dulles in the Office of Strategic Services.

*Schutzstaffel (*SS*).* Hitler's personal guard.

Schwarzer Peter. A card game.

*Sicherheitsdienst, Security Service (*SD*).* The intelligence division of the SS.

Spielschule. A literal translation is "play school."

Stauffenberg, Berthold (1905–1944). The older brother of Claus, he also took part in the failed coup attempt in Berlin that was underway after the assassination attempt on 20 July 1944. Executed 10 August 1944.

Stauffenberg, Claus (1907–1944). Career officer and colonel in the German Army. On 20 July 1944 he planted the explosives that were to kill Hitler at Wolfschanze. Stauffenberg then returned to Berlin where he attempted to carry out the planned coup. He was executed that same night.

Stein, Baron Karl von (1757–1831). Prussian statesman and chief minister of Prussia (1807–1808). He modernized the Prussian government and promoted self-government based on the English model.

*Sturmabteilung, Storm Troopers (*SA*).* Hitler's paramilitary organization.

Thompson, Dorothy (1894–1961). Famous American journalist. Hitler expelled her from Germany in 1934 after she began reporting on the Nazi movement.

Unter den Linden. Probably the most famous boulevard in Berlin, the Brandenburg Gate is located at its end. It is lined with linden trees.